The News and Public Opinion

Contemporary Political Communication

Max McCombs, R. Lance Holbert, Spiro Kiousis, Wayne Wanta, *The News and Public Opinion*

Craig Allen Smith, *Presidential Campaign Communication*

The News and Public Opinion

Media Effects on Civic Life

Max McCombs, R. Lance Holbert,
Spiro Kiousis, Wayne Wanta

polity

First published in 2011 by Polity Press

Polity Press
65 Bridge Street
Cambridge CB2 1UR, UK

Polity Press
350 Main Street
Malden, MA 02148, USA

ISBN-13: 978-0-7456-4518-6
ISBN-13: 978-0-7456-4519-3(pb)

A catalogue record for this book is available from the British Library.

Typeset in 11 on 13 pt Adobe Sabon
by Servis Filmsetting Ltd, Stockport, Cheshire

The publisher has used its best endeavours to ensure that the URLs for external websites referred to in this book are correct and active at the time of going to press. However, the publisher has no responsibility for the websites and can make no guarantee that a site will remain live or that the content is or will remain appropriate.

Every effort has been made to trace all copyright holders, but if any have been inadvertently overlooked the publisher will be pleased to include any necessary credits in any subsequent reprint or edition.

For further information on Polity, visit our website: www.politybooks.com

Contents

Introduction

What Is Public Opinion?

Public opinion often is narrowly regarded as the responses that people make to pollsters' questions about public affairs. The realities of public opinion are much more complex, involving a swirling, ever-changing mix of thoughts, feelings, and occasional behavior. The influences shaping this mix range from our childhood experiences to our most recent conversations. Especially prominent, however, is the steady succession of messages that we receive from the daily news. That is the focus of this book: the effects of the news media on the sequence of outcomes that collectively shape and define public opinion. The relationship between news media and public opinion is a dynamic process, and we examine in some detail each stage involved in this process that is so central to a well-functioning democracy.

How then do we define public opinion if it is more than just an utterance offered to a pollster? How have observers of public opinion come to understand this "swirling, ever-changing mix of thoughts, feelings, and occasional behavior"? As with many of communication and journalism's most important concepts (e.g., audience, media exposure), reaching consensus on a definition of public opinion has proved difficult. One approach to explicating this thorny concept is through disaggregation: that is, addressing its two primary components, public and opinion, largely separated from each other. A public, as opposed to a crowd or a mass, is a well-defined group with clear boundaries that actively engages in discourse about the major issues affecting the group. A primary goal of a public is the establishment of a reasonable consensus that allows for various decision-making processes to move forward while keeping the group intact over the long term. Importantly then, a public cannot consist of just one individual; as such, the formation of public opinion is a social and *communicative* process.

With consensus as a goal of a public, the notion of reaching consensus speaks directly to the concept of opinion. Opinion exists both within individuals who are part of a broader public and at the broader social level of the public as well. Observations of public opinion can occur and empirical data can be collected at both the individual and societal levels. Furthermore, public opinion can revolve around specific issues of the moment or can be thought of as the collective will of a society or nation. It also is particularly important to recognize that reaching consensus does not imply complete agreement on a topic, though it does suggest a majority view.

Opinions are both internally and socially constructed. For example, a citizen may form an opinion about a specific tax proposal based on his own personal concerns and self-interest. However, this individual's opinion about the tax proposal simultaneously will exist within and be influenced by a set of social forces that are far greater than the individual: the public's dominant values, worldviews, or political orientations. In short, an opinion should be viewed as complex and multidimensional.

Based on this discussion, public opinion can be broadly defined as *the collective consensus about political and civic matters reached by groups within larger communities*. And these groups, of course, can vary from very small entities to vast international groups and communities.

A particularly relevant dichotomy for understanding the concept of public opinion is a focus on *process* versus a focus on *outcomes*. Perspectives on public opinion as a process stress the role of dialogue and deliberation as core elements in the description and evaluation of public opinion. For example, Jürgen Habermas's concepts of communicative action and rational discourse underscore a diversity of voices as crucial elements in public opinion.[1] In contrast, perspectives stressing outcomes highlight public opinion as it is expressed through different forms of political participation and action. Dewey's vision of the New England town hall meeting, for instance, regards direct citizen participation in political decision-making as a core part of public opinion.[2] Our consideration of news and public opinion in this book embraces both perspectives in order to provide an expansive examination of their relationships.

Role of communication

Of fundamental importance to the focus of this book is the recognition that public opinion formation and change cannot exist without communication. There can be no public and there can be no opinion without communication. A public consists of individuals who communicate with one another about the major issues and topics of the day, and our opinions reflect what we wish to communicate to others about where we stand on these matters. Communication is a necessary but not sufficient condition for public opinion formation, and it is through the process of communication that consensus is reached in our civic life.

The chapters of this book discuss the range of cognitive, emotional, attitudinal, and behavioral outcomes associated with news consumption, outcomes that define the continuous evolution of democratic civic life. At the individual level, news has the potential to influence central democratic outcomes such as political knowledge. However, the effects of news are not purely cognitive. News media also have the ability to influence citizens' feelings toward a wide spectrum of political objects, ranging from entire branches of government, to specific pieces of legislation, to individuals seeking an elected political office. Indeed, public opinion is often most closely associated with citizens' attitudes. Pollsters commonly ask citizens to rate various political figures, such as the president of the United States, on a rating scale as a means for locating an individual's general attitude on a single continuum that ranges from extremely negative to extremely positive. In terms of observable civic behaviors, investigations of public opinion focus on much more than just voting. A broader range of inherently political activities are also important—for example, volunteering to work in a political campaign—along with a host of more indirect civic behaviors not directly related to politics (e.g., community volunteer activities), but which serve to aid various elements of democratic life.

Attention also will be given to the effects of news at the societal level. There are numerous inequities and problems in any society, and empirical studies of mass communication have wrestled with the question of whether news media content and the consumption of news by specific subpopulations serve to improve or exacerbate existing social ills. In addition, news media and their influence on public opinion can affect the making of public policy and the negotiations among elites that are at the heart of these processes. News media can also influence diplomatic efforts between countries by shaping how citizens in various countries come to view one another, bounding the efforts within which elites can function as they interact with one another globally (e.g., recent uprisings in Tunisia and Egypt). News plays a key role at the social level in regard to both core domestic and international affairs.

No assessment of media influence is complete without also surveying what individuals and societies bring to their mass media experiences. News media exposure is determined by a wide range of demographic variables, including age, income, and educational level. In addition, a number of psychological variables impact how much news individuals consume. Political orientations are also important elements in the role of news media in a citizen's daily life. Political party identification, political ideology, general political knowledge, and political interest all have been shown to be related, sometimes quite substantially, to diverse forms of news consumption. In addition, these political orientations have significant influences on how individuals create meaning from news stories as they approach politics from their own unique perspectives. It is imperative that this range of individual differences among citizens be properly accounted for in order to understand the nature of news media influence on the construction of public opinion within a democracy.

An overview

This book details the conditions under which the news produces a wide range of effects across diverse sets of individuals and subpopulations. We begin with an overview of the ever-moving evolution of the contemporary media landscape and an examination of the political messages found in the news media. Major contemporary trends in journalistic style and practice in the presentation of political news are detailed, as well as the longstanding and widely accepted normative standards for the practice of journalism in which these trends are grounded. These contemporary trends extend the realm of political communication far beyond the traditions of newspapers and television, and now include formats and media as disparate as blogs and political satire. From these overviews, we move to the heart of the book, an examination of the empirical social science evidence about the impact of journalism on the civic life of citizens. These media effects extend from simple awareness to behavioral outcomes. Finally, taking all these elements into account, we offer our judgment on how well today's news organizations are meeting the needs and expectations of democratic political life.

Our verdict on this point—and the exposition of media effects underpinning this verdict—will take into account the large array of voices in the contemporary media landscape. The emphasis, however, is not on the minute details of the ever-changing media landscape, but rather on the consistent impact over time that the mass media, whatever the medium, have on the thoughts, feelings, and behaviors that shape public opinion. The study of news media influence is fundamentally the study of process, and there are core processes of news media effects that have shaped, and that will continue to shape, public opinion for decades. These core processes of influence are the central story within which all media, new and old, function.

Elaborating a fundamental principle about the diffusion of new communication media in *MediaMorphosis: Understanding New Media*, Roger Fidler noted, "People do not buy information technologies—they buy content, usefulness, and convenience at the point when they perceive value to match the cost."[3] Although a variety of new media have eclipsed the market share of the older media in the marketplace of ideas, many aspects of political communication remain unchanged. More than half a century ago, Lazarsfeld and colleagues observed that voters who were heavy users of one news medium tended to be heavy users of other news media as well.[4] At that time, the focus was primarily on newspapers and radio, but that pattern still prevailed three decades later when newspapers and television were the dominant political voices. To take another, more recent example of media convergence, the media agendas of issues available to citizens now use both online and traditional media. These news agendas remain essentially as homogeneous today, however, as they were four decades ago during the golden age of television and newspapers. Any effort to paint the political effects of the contemporary media landscape in terms of its specific and evolving technologies would be obsolete before the first reader opens this book. But the knowledge gained about the collective impact of the news media on the formation of public opinion will be viable for all readers of this book.

Public opinion is manifested in many ways, from private conversations to very public actions, such as voting on Election Day or parading in support of a particular stand on an issue. In all of its many manifestations, public opinion is influenced by the news media. This status was recognized more than a century ago by British observer James Bryce in his classic *The American Commonwealth*,[5] and by French sociologist Gabriel Tarde,[6] whose analysis of the public opinion process identified the news media as the prime movers for conversation, opinion, and action. The effects of news on public opinion can take many different forms and result from many different paths of influence.

These media effects can be direct or indirect. Exposure to a specific news item may lead directly to the creation of a new level of awareness by an individual audience member about some emerging public issue. Subsequent thinking about the issue stimulated by the news story may result in a face-to-face discussion of the issue by the individual. In this case, news exposure had an indirect influence on political discussion through the mediating variable of deliberation. It is important to recognize, however, that identifying the direct versus indirect effects of news on public opinion is not an either-or scenario. There is the potential for news to have multiple direct and indirect influences on various democratic outcomes simultaneously. It is most important for journalism to take an expansive view of news media influence on public opinion, a perspective going beyond just those effects that can be defined as direct.

Just as it is important to look at the direct and indirect effects of news media, there is also a need to consider unintended as well as intended effects. An obvious intended effect of news is the diffusion of political knowledge among the electorate. Journalists gather various pieces of information and organize that information in order to tell a story with the express purpose of communicating a specific perspective about current situations and events, and these new pieces of information can shape public opinion. But not all of the effects of the news on public opinion are intended. A host of unintended effects of news have been identified through empirical research. For example, consistent results from research on the knowledge gap hypothesis reveal that increased consumption of news by individuals who have high socioeconomic status serves to widen the gap between society's "haves" and "have nots" when it comes to their understanding of core political processes. Widening the knowledge gap between persons with high and low socioeconomic status is not the intention of most news media organizations.

Other unintended effects include the polarization of attitudes resulting from selective exposure that reinforces and strengthens previously held opinions, and the creation of a spiral of silence in which some individuals fall silent because of a fear that their opinions do not match majority opinion. Although unintended, such effects exist, and it is important that we consider both intended and unintended effects in our understanding of the relationship between news and public opinion.

In our time, social scientists have mapped this influence of the news on public opinion in great detail. Our emphasis here is on the basic principles of communication established by these investigations into the elements shaping public opinion, beginning with initial attention to the various news media and their contents and extending to the acquisition of information and opinions and to the consequences of all these elements for participation in public life.

I

The News Media

1

A Changing Communication Environment

Although there is debate from time to time about the extent of influence that the news has across a range of democratic outcomes, there is little disagreement that there has been profound change in the news media landscape during the past decade. Where previous generations were considered well connected to public affairs if they had access to several TV networks' national news broadcasts and their local affiliates' coverage, a public broadcasting outlet, a local daily newspaper, as well as newsmagazines and news/talk-formatted radio stations, today's news consumer can access literally thousands of public affairs outlets with relative ease and at little to no cost.

It is important to place these changes of recent years in their proper context because this changing media landscape has altered how citizens engage in democracy. Moreover, access to a much larger number of news outlets should not be assumed to be an inherent good. Markus Prior has argued that the overall increase in media outlets seen in recent years has created an audience largely made up of two classes, news junkies and news avoiders.[1] News junkies represent only 10–15 percent of the population, and these individuals thrive in the rapidly evolving news media landscape, whereas the far larger group of avoiders finds it all the easier to bypass more traditional forms of news altogether. News avoiders may have come into contact with news in the past only incidentally, but they can now evade the news almost altogether given the range of entertainment media options that are continually at their disposal.

The rise of the internet also has brought a profound set of changes to news organizations, and the presentation of news at the local, state, national, and international levels has been permanently altered. For local and state news, most daily newspapers have a web presence that offers a varying balance of original content with a repetition of the information that can be found in the traditional print version of the paper. At the national level, all the news organizations with national reputations are but a click away for most media consumers. Daily online versions of *The New York Times*, *The Washington Post*, the *Los Angeles Times*, and many other respected news organizations can become part of almost anyone's daily news routine.

In addition, it is equally possible for selected local news coverage to supplant national news coverage depending on the issues of the day. Consider Senator John McCain's choice of Governor Sarah Palin of Alaska to be his running mate for the 2008 U.S. presidential election. Palin was at the time a relative unknown on the national stage, but was much better known in her home state of Alaska. A citizen could read or watch what national reporters from NBC News, *The New York Times*, or even *The Dallas Morning News* had to say about Palin, but this citizen also may have found it fruitful to go straight to the web version of the *Anchorage Daily News* to see exactly what was being said in Alaska about this surprise nomination. With access to the web, a citizen can gather this type of information rather easily.

Finally, the shrinking of the globe as a result of the rise of the web can be felt most profoundly at the international level. Whereas in the past only the most elite within a society had access to even a small range of international news outlets, even the average citizen can now gain instant access to public affairs outlets across the globe that offer vastly different perspectives on the major issues of the day. This is not only true of citizens of the West gaining access to news outlets from the Middle East and East Asia, just to offer one example, but citizens from the other areas of the globe now have better access to Western media perspectives as well.

This chapter will first outline the present state of the traditional news media: newspapers, television, and radio. Recent changes in these traditional news outlets such as the rise of cable TV news will be reviewed. The rise of the web also will be detailed in the context of how traditional news outlets have reacted to the rise of digital media as important information channels for citizens. Finally, there are the entertainment-based outlets that also offer audiences political information. There is much debate as to whether these entertainment outlets, such as *The Daily Show with Jon Stewart*, *The Colbert Report*, and *The Onion*, should be considered news outlets as well.[2] There also has been considerable discussion concerning their overall influence on basic democratic processes.[3] No matter where one's position falls within these debates, it is essential that these outlets be examined in line with all the other changes taking place in the news media landscape.

Traditional news outlets

Newspapers

It is no secret that the average daily newspaper has been in steady decline in terms of readership and profitability for several decades. In 2006 the Pew Research Center for People and the Press found that only about 40 percent of those surveyed regularly read a daily newspaper. This percentage shrunk to 34 percent when those individuals who only read the print version of the daily newspaper were isolated from the rest of the respondents. This 2006 percentage of daily readership was down a full 18 points from 1994 levels, and those 1994 levels were already a reflection of a steep decline in readership that had occurred during the 1980s and early 1990s. Back in 1970, daily newspaper readership was estimated to be 78 percent of the American population by the Newspaper Association of America. In short, newspapers have been in perilous decline for many decades, and there is solid empirical evidence that new generations of readers are not replacing the older generations that once treated reading the newspaper as one of their daily rituals.[4]

What is the root cause for this decline? Part of the issue is shifting demographics and changing lifestyle patterns. Younger adults simply are not turning to the daily print-based newspaper in the numbers seen in previous generations. Age alone does not explain this steep readership decline, however. Other demographic factors matter, with gender and race being relatively important players in this story. Women and minorities are less likely to read a daily newspaper.

A recent Readership Institute survey also notes that readers of a daily newspaper especially want local news in their newspapers, the type of local coverage that is difficult to get through any other information source.[5] As a result, Stepp contends that when newspapers cut back their local reporting staff due to budgetary constraints and replace local coverage with more wire service–generated content, they are sealing their own fate in terms of readership. The Readership Institute survey also points to the need for radical innovations by the industry to create the type of content that will attract a younger, more ethnically diverse audience. Too many daily newspapers are still using traditional formatting, which simply does not speak to some of the media industry's most desired demographics, such as younger males and minorities.

The newspaper industry is fighting what amounts to a two-front war, with a dual focus on stemming its loss of readers for the traditional print edition while establishing a well-defined presence online. Most daily newspapers offer some type of web presence, but the movement to a new medium has not been easy. In the early 1990s, newspapers rushed to put content on the internet, usually employing "shovelware" to reproduce verbatim on the web the content originally created for the print edition. This happened because journalists viewed the internet as an extension of the old medium instead of a new communication tool.

Shortly after the turn of the century, however, many media organizations started offering more diverse content, including audio and video clips as well as an increased number of interactive elements. Many online sites also concentrate more on local news and information in comparison to their newspapers' print editions. This effort to offer original content on the web, information that is distinct from what can be found in the print edition of the newspaper, reflects a desire to embrace the instantaneous nature of the web and provide up-to-date news and information to the audience. Both elements are important in order to be effective on the web. The web affords news organizations an opportunity to create content that is more interactive, allowing audience members the experience of engaging news content in ways that far surpass anything that could be offered through a traditional print-based medium. In addition, audience members have come to expect new, constantly updated information when they turn to a news-oriented web site. There is no deadline with the web—it is constantly feeding on new content. If newspaper organizations are not willing or able to post constant updates to their web sites, then many readers will fail to become regular consumers of these web sites. In turn, the constant deadline that comes with the web has become a significant tension for traditional news organizations that are used to working with set deadlines.

For many newspaper organizations the web has created new possibilities to expand readership. This is particularly true for newspapers with established reputations that far exceed their traditional geographic reach. For example, *The New York Times* and *The Washington Post* have long had worldwide reputations as news organizations that provide sound reporting on the major issues of the day. With their web versions, these two news organizations are able to reach a level of readership that matches their reputation. It is just as easy for me to connect to *The New York Times* online if I am in Tokyo, Auckland, Moscow, London, or Paris as if I were in New York City and its surrounding metropolitan areas. This point speaks to distribution even more than form or content. The web offers newspaper organizations a cheaper, more efficient means to reach potential consumers. This new form of distribution provides a tool to try to reestablish lost readership in a particular area, as well as to establish an expanded audience that reaches far beyond what was feasible through more traditional modes of distribution—physically loading newspapers on trucks and distributing them to carriers who travel around neighborhoods throwing the printed paper on driveways or front lawns.

Another recent trend is the availability of podcasts, internet files that listeners can download to a computer and transfer to an MP3 player. One estimate claimed that 55 million people have already subscribed to a podcast by 2010. Podcasts are now available through such news media as the *Washington Post, The New York Times, Wall Street Journal,* ABC, CBS, NBC, and their affiliates. Podcasts offer several advantages, including time-shifting capabilities, portability, and self-expressiveness. Podcast production is also inexpensive, meaning that they can be produced by amateurs.

Regardless of how people get news from the web, this medium has become a dominant channel of communication and has passed newspapers as a primary source of public affairs news and information.

Television

The days of the three major television networks' dominance in the United States are long past. A precipitous drop in ratings for the major evening network newscasts has vastly changed the dynamics of the networks' news divisions. Although the U.S. audience for an average nightly newscast can reach upwards of 8 million viewers, the percentage of potential viewers turning to these presentations of public affairs information has been steadily dropping for many years. This loss in audience share has brought with it a loss of profitability and a loss of power. The news divisions at NBC, ABC, and CBS are now much more likely to make decisions about what they present based on softer forms of news and infotainment, such as NBC's *The Today Show* or ABC's *Good Morning America,* rather than in terms of hard news. It is the softer forms of "news" programming that are most profitable, and profitability drives corporate media in America.

Another key issue with traditional broadcast news is the demographics of who is still tuning in to watch the nightly news. Age is a very strong predictor of who is in the audience, with those who are older watching the most. The problem is that the older populations watching national network TV news are not being replaced with a more youthful demographic. In addition, there remains a solid gender gap—men tend to watch more television news than women. Hiring Katie Couric, a younger woman who made her name in morning soft news, to anchor the *CBS Evening News* is a good example of the efforts by the major television networks to signal change to the American public. Hiring a younger woman can appeal to both the gender and youth gaps in the nightly network news audience.

The most important changes to television news are not in the broadcast realm, but in cable television. Cable TV news really came of age during the first Gulf War in 1990–1991. In particular, CNN's around-the-clock coverage of this international crisis created a news dynamic not offered by the major television networks. The war coverage on CNN was constant, and audience members could tune in whenever they wished to get an up-to-date assessment about what was happening in the Gulf or with the major international players involved in the war. CNN gained a tremendous amount of credibility with its coverage of the war, and the result was a fundamental shift by a significant percentage of the American television news audience from broadcast news to cable TV news.

CNN may have paved the way for cable TV news becoming a legitimate provider of public affairs information, but Fox News has taken this window of opportunity and devised a presentation of news that does not match anything else found in television. Fox News was created to appeal to a specific audience that falls along ideological lines. Its choice of which stories to cover and the way in which these issues are framed reflect a conservative political ideology.[6] Fox News has been able to establish a loyal audience base by taking this approach, and the existence of this outlet on cable television packages has served the Republican Party of the United States well by providing a platform for conservative politicians' issues and agendas.

Getlin, for instance, found that Fox News coverage of the Iraq War was more pro-war and pro-military than other media coverage.[7] Deggans quotes Fox anchor Neil Cavuto as arguing that he saw nothing wrong with taking sides in covering a war. This pro-war stance has an effect on viewers.[8] Christopher Beaudoin and colleagues found that Fox News viewers were more likely to support the Iraq War than other news consumers.[9]

Jonathan Morris also found differences between Fox News viewers and other news consumers.[10] Viewers of Fox News had distinct voting patterns, a distinct set of political attitudes toward President George W. Bush, and a view of political reality different from other news consumers. Morris argues that these differences could point toward further political polarization among U.S. citizens as differences among television news programs become more pronounced. An earlier study by Morris found that Fox viewers were also less informed than other television news viewers.[11] Fox viewers underestimated the number of American casualties in the Iraq War and were less likely to follow stories critical of the Bush Administration.

Some argue that other cable TV news organizations are beginning to follow Fox's lead, seeking to find their own ideological niche within the cable television news audience. Most notably, MSNBC became a clear combatant of Fox News during the 2008 general election season with its own brand of more liberally oriented content, such as *The Rachel Maddow Show*.

In addition, cable television news is no longer just about politics and the clashing of various political perspectives. A major component of cable television news deals with financial issues. This movement toward more cable TV news content devoted to business and finance makes sense given the changing nature of the relationship between the American stock market and the general public. The retirement accounts and pensions of a larger percentage of Americans are closely tied to the daily ups and downs of the stock market. As a result, the audience for business and financial news has increased exponentially in recent years. Business and financial news is no longer the privilege of the elite—it has become a much more egalitarian concern. Television, being an egalitarian medium, has followed suit in providing coverage of these topics.

Radio

Public affairs content on radio has to do much more with opinion than the traditional reporting of news. The major change in the realm of radio is the rise of conservative talk programs.[12] This revolution has many players, but the dominant voice is Rush Limbaugh, who has a clear ideological bent and proclivity for all things conservative. Radio offers a format that fits well with the conservative message, with several other radio show hosts such as Michael Savage and Sean Hannity able to establish a solid audience base for their equally conservative content. The liberal wing's attempt to create a counterpresence, *Air America*, has not been able to establish a strong voice in this medium when compared to Limbaugh, Hannity, and Savage. In short, the medium of radio is clearly leaning in one ideological direction.

Satellite radio also offers a variety of news and public-affairs information outlets. Several news outlets such as CNN and Fox News are strongly present in satellite radio, and there are distinct news channels that exist in satellite radio as well: POTUS, for example. Satellite radio is struggling to gain an audience sufficient to become self-sustaining and profitable, but even so it is a medium where a tremendous amount of news and public-affairs information can be distributed.

Radio also is the one place where publicly funded, not-for-profit news has been able to establish a presence in America. National Public Radio (NPR) is a much more significant player in radio than the Public Broadcasting Service (PBS) is in television. Publicly funded media have always been minor players in the American media model, in contrast to many other countries, but in radio publicly funded stations have been able to produce quality news content on a large scale. NPR's flagship programs, *Morning Edition* and *All Things Considered* in the early evening, rank high in their quality and size of audience among broadcast news programs.

The ideological changes in radio and television could be attributed to the natural evolution of communication media. Merrill and Lowenstein argue that media go through three stages in their evolution: Elite, Popular, and Specialized.[13] When a medium is first introduced into society, it is typically aimed at the elite. Magazines, for example, were edited for the elite when they emerged in the 1800s. The elites were the only social class that knew how to read. Next, a medium is oriented toward the masses and becomes popular with most individuals in society. Again, magazines provide a good example. In the 1900s, mass-circulation magazines such as *Life* and the *Saturday Evening Post* dominated the magazine market for roughly the first half of the century. Finally, a medium evolves and becomes specialized. In the magazine industry, we do not have broadly focused pet magazines or dog magazines, but rather magazines such as the *Aussie Times*, aimed specifically at owners of Australian Shepherds.

Early radio content also was aimed at the elite, since they were the only social class who could afford to buy a radio. Then, radio became popular with the masses, with serials, music, and general entertainment programming. Eventually, radio became specialized, so that we now have music stations focusing on a wide variety of genres, from classical music to classic rock. Radio, however, could be entering an even more specialized stage. Not only are there radio stations devoted to news, but some radio stations are devoted to talk news—content in which listeners interact with radio commentators. But these talk news stations are even becoming specialized, with conservative commentators and liberal commentators. These commentators often attract listeners by being sensational "shock jocks." The content of these news talk programs tends to be extreme and one-sided, a trend that could be an influence on the polarization of political attitudes that is currently evident in the United States.[14]

Entertainment-based public affairs

The rise of entertainment media with coverage and discussion of public affairs has been a major phenomenon in recent years. We have even reached the point where there is discussion in the traditional press of Jon Stewart, host of Comedy Central's *The Daily Show*, being the most trusted personality in journalism.[15] In addition to *The Daily Show with Jon Stewart*, a host of other entertainment-oriented television programs regularly make headlines with their coverage of American politics. These programs include *The Colbert Report* on Comedy Central, the political segments offered on *Saturday Night Live,* and the monologues of Jay Leno, David Letterman, and many other late-night talk show hosts who regularly critique political figures using humor.[16] In addition, there is the more hard-hitting political fare offered on premium cable television channels, with *Real Time with Bill Maher* being one of the most popular programs.

One line of debate concerning much of this content centers around whether it is proper to discuss this entertainment-based material in the same way we would approach mainstream journalism and reporting. Some have argued that the type of material offered on *The Daily Show with Jon Stewart* is a new type of journalism,[17] but others have scoffed at this notion and highlight some of the potential democratic downsides such as cynicism that come with the broader themes offered by Jon Stewart and other satirists.[18]

A number of different forces have been at work to create this unusual chapter in the history of journalism and its relationship to entertainment-based content. The first concerns the audience. More specifically, younger generations have been identified as particularly susceptible to treating *The Daily Show* and other programs of its kind as news. Some have argued that younger voters are getting most or all of their public affairs information from these entertainment-based outlets. However, even young voters see clear conceptual distinctions between a program like *The Daily Show* and more traditional forms of television news in terms of political gratifications.[19] In addition, there is little evidence that programming such as *The Daily Show* is competing with traditional news as a source of public affairs news and information among young voters. Younger citizens tend to use entertainment-based public affairs programming in coordination with, not as a replacement of, more traditional forms of news.[20]

One potential reason for the vaunted status of some types of entertainment content within the context of public affairs is that the present practice of journalism is so poor. This is the argument most often used by Jon Stewart himself when asked why his program is more and more defined as journalism. Just as some entertainment content has been presented more like news, so too news has become more like entertainment programming in recent years. Some content analyses show that *The Daily Show* rivals many news organizations in terms of the level of substantive material it offers concerning political campaigns.[21] If traditional news is not any more substantive than *The Daily Show* in its coverage of politics, then it is not the fault of Jon Stewart or the media audience that this program is being brought into the fold of journalism. The blame rests more squarely with news media organizations themselves, and the rise of *The Daily Show* as a news outlet may be an unintended byproduct of news trying to be more entertainment-oriented in its effort to attract or at least retain audience share.

Building on this point, public trust of news media institutions remains very low at this moment in time.[22] It may not be that Jon Stewart is rising in legitimacy, but that the news media are sinking to such a low level of public trust that some types of entertainment programming can now be classified as just as legitimate as other news organizations. It is especially important to note, however, that the news media of the past were not the focus of such a relentless assault on their credibility as the news media have been in recent years. They are a constant focus of mockery for many of the most popular satirists found in today's media environment.[23] In addition, conservative media outlets have made the "elite news corps" a constant target of their derision.[24] Finally, the degree and harshness by which politicians now blame the press for failings in the political realm is unprecedented.[25] It is clear that one outcome of these multiple lines of attack has been a decrease in trust in the news media among the American public. However, this does not mean that the news media themselves are not partly to blame for the public's loss of trust. It is rarely the case that a single culprit is at work when such a dramatic shift in public opinion occurs.

Finally, the fact that many types of entertainment media are now mentioned in the same breath as news may be due in part to the political elite. The 1992 U.S. presidential election was the first concerted effort by major political party campaigns to bypass journalists as filters in an effort to get their unadulterated messages to voters through various entertainment outlets such as late-night talk shows.[26] The fact that major politicians became regular guests on programs of this kind instilled a sense of legitimacy the programs had not enjoyed previously. It has reached the point where some politicians have gone so far as to announce their presidential aspirations on programs such as *The Daily Show with Jon Stewart*, as former senator and vice-presidential candidate John Edwards did so to start his campaign for the 2008 Democratic presidential nomination. In short, there are many potential causes for why entertainment media content and traditional news are beginning to be discussed as equals in the realm of politics.

Much of the discussion about entertainment-based media relative to news has focused on television. Satirical material on politics can be found in other media forms as well, however. *The Onion* is a classic example of a highly popular satirical outlet that uses a variety of media forms outside of television. *The Onion* began in print form in Madison, Wisconsin, but has now become a true multimedia national entity. This satirical outlet also exists on the web, boasts the release of a full-length feature film, *The Onion Movie*, and produces regular streaming audio that can be consumed in a variety of ways ranging from satellite radio to podcasts. It is interesting to note that satirical outlets such as *The Onion* have joined forces with traditional news outlets such as washingtonpost.com. Audience members can now see at the bottom of most washingtonpost.com articles a listing of URL links to "our [washingtonpost.com's] partner, *The Onion*." If *The Washington Post* for a time defined *The Onion*, a satirical news outlet, as a "partner," this speaks loudly about how closely wedded traditional news and entertainment media have become in today's media environment.

All of the entertainment outlets highlighted so far involve the use of humor. The concept of news has expanded, however, to include soft news—for example, *Entertainment Tonight*, a non-humorous form of media entertainment content.[27] Baum found that a considerable amount of public-affairs material is presented on these types of programs and that consumption of this kind of media content has effects on a wide range of democratic outcomes, from gains in political knowledge to shifts in political attitudes. In addition, Baum's gateway hypothesis posits that consumption of this soft news with public-affairs content creates a greater likelihood that audience members will seek out some type of traditional news. Information gained from soft news can prime viewers to the importance of some political issues and provide them with some degree of knowledge about the topic at hand, outcomes that allow greater accessibility for hard news information. Parallel to Young and Tisinger's claim that late-night comedy television and traditional news should be viewed as complements of each other,[28] so too does Baum's gateway hypothesis point to soft news and hard news forming a complementary relationship.

Finally, it is important to note that major motion pictures are beginning to take on journalistic roles in their presentation of political issues. A prime example of this phenomenon is Michael Moore's controversial documentary *Fahrenheit 9/11*, distributed across the country in the middle of the 2004 U.S. presidential election. In this film, Moore presented previously unreported documents concerning George W. Bush and his term of duty in the U.S. National Guard. Moore detailed in the film how he came to possess these documents, and he also outlined a degrees-of-separation argument for how the Bush family was closely tied to the Bin Laden family. A series of studies by Holbert, Hansen, and colleagues revealed a complex set of political effects stemming from this film. Viewing the film worked in coordination with viewing other campaign-related events, such as a political debate, to influence voters' political attitudes toward the two major party candidates, Bush and John Kerry.[29] Moore was clearly engaging in journalistic activities in gathering material for his one-sided, anti-Bush film.

It is clear that we need to include films like *Fahrenheit 9/11* when we discuss the state of journalism in the new media landscape. Other media organizations claiming to be "fair and balanced," such as Fox News, engage in activities that are not all that different from what Michael Moore does when making a political film.

Conclusion

There have been extreme changes in the news media landscape during the past decade. First, there are the major alterations in the traditional news media. Some media are clearly hurting, particularly daily newspapers and broadcast TV, and are attempting to revitalize themselves with the assistance of the web. Other media are becoming much more diverse in the type of public affairs content being offered, with more and more outlets becoming sources for partisan material. Cable TV and radio are prime examples. No matter the cause, there are profound changes at play with traditional news media outlets, and change will be the constant for the coming years. In addition, traditional journalists are using every new digital technology application at their disposal to disseminate news content. And as digital technologies continue to expand and evolve, the channels of communication that journalists will have at their disposal to report on the major issues of the day will increase exponentially.

Finally, there is much discussion surrounding the root causes for why entertainment is becoming more like news and news is becoming more like entertainment. The age of media convergence has brought together media genres that used to be seen as quite disparate. Diana Mutz has argued that it is futile to speak of a distinction between news and entertainment within the present media landscape because it is increasingly difficult to tell where the news begins and the entertainment ends and vice versa.[30] This will become all the more the case in the coming years. To paraphrase a popular automobile advertising slogan from a few years ago, "This isn't your daddy's news media environment."

2

Reporting the News

On the surface, journalists have a simple job. They gather information, organize it in a logical fashion using proper grammar and style, and then transmit the information through a medium that is accessible to consumers. Gather, produce, send—it sounds all too easy. The job of journalists, however, is much more complicated. There are numerous obstacles to overcome, including influences from a variety of sources and organizational pressures from within and outside news organizations. These pressures form a hierarchy of influence: five levels of influence on the news extending outward from journalists' backgrounds to their job routines, their media organization, outside influences, and the social and cultural setting in which they work.

Journalists have ultimate control over their news content, however. They act as "gatekeepers"—allowing some content to filter through to the public while holding back other content. Kurt Lewin[1] was the first to use the term "gatekeeping." A sociologist, he used the term to describe a process of how food purchasing decisions affected social change. Various members of the population differed in their influence on what was eaten by others, and "gatekeeping" was used to refer to the decisions of the people who transported, bought, and prepared food.

David Manning White[2] used the concept of gatekeeping to describe the news production process of a wire editor at a daily newspaper. White noted that "Mr. Gates" rejected some stories because they were "not interesting," "B.S.," or because he didn't care for such stories, and he concluded that the decision-making process was "highly subjective." In short, personal background was regarded as a major factor in gatekeeping.

Extensive examinations of journalists' backgrounds in the United States[3] have found that the typical journalist tends to be male, Protestant, liberal, college-educated and middle-class. Journalists typically do not see themselves as passive disseminators of factual information, but instead view their roles as active interpreters of what is news. The personal backgrounds of journalists can play a role in how journalists do their jobs, though most journalists will claim news selection is based on newsworthiness and journalists' professional instincts.[4]

Overall, story selection is influenced far more by journalistic routines than by the individual characteristics of staff writers and editors.[5] The way that journalists do their job very much influences news content. Journalists gather information and report the news based on a series of steps learned through their education in journalism programs and their experiences in the newsroom. These news routines are ingrained in a journalist's psyche. Because journalists rarely witness news events first-hand, they must locate information through knowledgeable and efficient news sources. In addition, journalists employ news-gathering strategies aimed at demonstrating that the journalist's account is balanced and unbiased. One of the most common is selecting sources who represent distinctly opposite perspectives on a topic. This can result, however, in presenting complex issues as simple dichotomies rather than ranges of opinions. Sociologist Gaye Tuchman[6] refers to this process as "objectivity as strategic ritual" in which journalists claim objectivity in order to defend their stories from critics.

Routines provide a certain comfort level for journalists. They cover the news today the same way they covered the news yesterday. An over-reliance on news routines causes three problems for reporters. First, news routines tend to influence reporters to cover events rather than issues. It is easier to cover an event—such as a murder trial—rather than an underlying issue—such as causes of crime within a city. Second, news routines tend to cause reporters to rely heavily on public officials. A city council member is easier to track down than private citizens with relevant information, who are more difficult to identify and locate. Finally, routines can lead to "pack journalism" in which reporters cover stories in nearly identical ways. News media have made numerous efforts to break from the stale reporting style inherent in rigid adherence to news routines. Some media have changed their beat structure, while others have attempted some form of public journalism, which will be detailed later in this chapter.

Media organizations also affect the news product. Journalists cannot write anything that they want. Media organizations have standards. News directors and editors in these organizations have both implicit and explicit influence on their reporters. This organizational influence on journalists was noted by Warren Breed, who argued that journalists face constraints resulting from the structure of management and ownership within their place of employment.[7] A newly hired journalist, through observation and discussion with co-workers, learns quickly what is acceptable and unacceptable on the job. Journalists want to be rewarded with raises and good assignments, so they try to please their superiors by conforming to newsroom standards, a process that Breed calls socialization in the newsroom. James Hamilton, for instance, argues that ownership of news organizations by companies with interests in other businesses can affect news coverage.[8] Journalists may be tempted to boost the parent company with positive news coverage of its other ventures.

Looking at the market served by a media organization, H. Shik Kim found differences between network and local television journalists in their selection patterns of international news.[9] International stories selected by network journalists demonstrated a global view with diverse themes. Local television journalists, in contrast, chose international stories with a local angle, perhaps because of local audience demands and business pressures.

The final two levels in this hierarchy of influence involve pressure from outside, such as advertisers and news sources, and the impact of the social environment. Media organizations are businesses, and they must make money to survive. Advertisers and consumers, through their monetary support of the media, can affect content. Moreover, hegemony theorists believe media organizations have a vested interest in maintaining the status quo in society. Media organizations seek to maximize profit and therefore provide only content that they think is deemed acceptable and appropriate based on societal norms. Although journalists are largely unaware that they are taking part in this process, society does influence media content in this way.

Todd Gitlin argues that hegemony was at work in the news coverage of student demonstrations during the Vietnam War.[10] He defines hegemony as "the ruling class's domination of subordinate classes and groups through the elaboration and penetration of ideology into their common sense and everyday practice." Coverage focused on minor aspects of the demonstrations as singular events rather than on the larger message behind the protests.

Arguably, one of the most important external influences on the news is the president of the United States. Wayne Wanta and colleagues examined the influence that presidents had on the news media agenda through their State of the Union addresses.[11] The findings were mixed, with President Nixon influencing subsequent media coverage and President Carter being influenced by previous media coverage. President Reagan, meanwhile, influenced newspaper coverage, but appears to have been influenced by television news. Certainly, many factors were at play here. All in all, the news reports presented to the public represent a complex confluence of influences.

Media influence

The hierarchy-of-influences approach gives rise to two questions. First, if there are these various influences on media content, what exactly in the media content is being influenced? Second, do the outcomes of these influences on the news demonstrate an overt bias among journalists and media?

There are numerous areas of routine media coverage that are susceptible to influences from both inside and outside media organizations. These include:

- **Issues and people, or what gets covered.** Journalists can show a personal bias just by the topics they choose to cover.
- **Framing of issues and people, or what aspects of stories get covered.** For example, the global warming issue is often framed as an economic issue (hardships on businesses to stop pollution) rather than an environmental issue (climate change causing serious weather pattern problems).
- **The tone, or how positive or negative the coverage is.** Readers will get a different impression of a political candidate depending on whether the candidate is shown to be a strong leader or someone who pushes a narrow agenda.
- **Sources used, or who gets quoted in stories.** Reporters often rely on public officials as sources because they are available, they have name recognition and thus give credibility to stories, and they have well-known opinion stances, so reporters know ahead of time what type of quotes they will get.
- **How someone gets quoted.** Quotes can be taken out of context, creating an impression that can be counter to the original intent of a source.
- **Visual content.** Photographers have two goals: capturing the most significant "frozen moment of reality" or capturing the unusual. Which gets used with accompanying stories can lead to entirely different reactions from readers.
- **Story placement.** A front-page story will be viewed as more important than a story appearing on an inside page. Front-page placement gives readers the impression that a story is highly important. Stories on inside pages are less of a priority.
- **Choice of words.** Many words have hidden meanings and different connotations. For example, a reporter could use the verb "said" with a source's quote, which carries a neutral meaning. But the reporter also could use the verb "claimed," which leads to the impression that the source might or might not be accurate.

Obviously, these choices can, by concentrating on certain aspects while ignoring others, have significant influence on news consumers. Thus public opinion can be greatly influenced through the shaping of media content. This situation is inevitable given the nature of the journalistic profession. The process of gathering, producing, and sending news will require these types of choices to be made, and the attributions people make in association with the various decisions made by journalists and news organizations will vary widely.

Media bias

Journalists have long been criticized for being biased. Many critics claim the news media have a liberal bias and favor the Democratic Party. An equally large and vocal group of critics, however, believe the media have a conservative bias and have been timidly following Republican public officials. On the other hand, some researchers have found no liberal or conservative bias in the news. Indeed, researchers have found support for all three of these possibilities. One reason for the mixed results is that much of the research in support of media bias—both on the right and the left—is anecdotal. The fact is that true objectivity is impossible, meaning that instances of bias occur every day, though liberally biased stories are often balanced out with conservatively biased stories.

This question of media bias is especially important for public opinion. There is evidence, for example, that partisan support for candidates on the editorial pages of newspapers can influence voting behavior.[12] What about a partisan tilt in the news?

Liberal bias

Critics claiming the media have a liberal bias often point to the fact that more reporters are registered as Democrats and identify themselves as liberals than are registered as Republicans and identify themselves as conservatives.[13] Jim Kuypers argues that the news media often do not cover the president's key messages fully and accurately. Using the example of a speech by President Bush, he criticizes the media for blaming a bad economy on the president while ignoring evidence to the contrary.[14]

Stephen Farnsworth and Robert Lichter found conflicting results in their examination of *The New York Times* and *The Washington Post*.[15] The *Times'* coverage of Congress leaned toward the Democrats, while the *Post* provided a more balanced view. They also found differences across topic coverage. The *Post* coverage was highly positive on Republicans when job performance was analyzed separately. The tone of most coverage in both papers regardless of political party, however, was negative. Adam Schiffer examined whether local newspapers showed a liberal bias in their coverage of political candidates and found "a modest amount of residual slant toward the Democratic candidates."[16]

Conservative bias

Counter to the claims of a liberal bias in the media, Eric Alterman argues that the news media have consciously moved toward the right.[17] His claims are supported by Geoffrey Numberg, who examined whether U.S. senators were labeled as being liberal or conservative. He found that a liberal senator has a 30 percent greater chance of being labeled than a conservative senator. However, he believes that labeling is due more to a senator's celebrity than to ideology. He notes that well-known liberals and conservatives such as Ted Kennedy and Jesse Helms are often labeled as a way of reassuring readers that the media are in the center and far from the extremes of the right or left.[18]

No bias

As David Weaver and G. Cleveland Wilhoit note, journalists tend to be liberal while editors tend to be conservative, creating a political balance in the newsroom.[19] Thus, the organizational structure of the newsrooms, coupled with the professional standards of journalists, make it highly unlikely that any one political philosophy will dominate. David Niven, for instance, found no evidence of a liberal or conservative bias in coverage of Presidents Bill Clinton and George H. W. Bush, concluding that allegations of a pro-liberal media are unfounded. He did, however, find that the news media report on bad outcomes of presidents' actions more often than good outcomes.[20]

A comprehensive meta-analysis also suggests very limited bias on the part of the news media. Dave D'Alessio and Mike Allen examined three types of bias: gatekeeping bias, editors' selection patterns from a pool of potential news content; coverage bias, coverage of an issue or event that is unbalanced; and statement bias, when journalists insert personal opinions in news stories. Their analysis of previous research shows no evidence of bias in gatekeeping or coverage. They did, however, find limited support for a statement bias that was pro-Republican in newsmagazines and pro-Democratic for television network news. Newspapers showed no statement bias.[21]

Nonetheless, the fact is that many people on both sides of the political spectrum perceive a bias in the media. This has led to studies examining the "hostile media effect," in which individuals perceive the media to be biased against their political views, regardless of whether they are conservative or liberal. And the majority of Americans do view the media to have a political bias. A 2003 Gallup poll found that 45 percent of Americans believe the news media to be too liberal while 14 percent believe the media are too conservative.

The cause of the hostile media effect is unclear. Mark Watts, David Domke, Dhavan Shah, and David Fan, in their analysis of the 1988, 1992, and 1996 U.S. presidential elections, argue that the rise in public perception that news media are liberally biased can be explained by increased news coverage that concentrates on the topic of bias in news content and is not the result of actual partisan bias.[22] The increased perceptions of media bias mainly come from conservatives who criticize the entire media industry as having a liberal bias.

Kathleen Schmitt, Albert Gunther, and Janice Liebhart identified three possible causes for the hostile media effect: selective recall, in which partisans remember only certain aspects of coverage that is opposed to their own side; selective categorization, in which partisans assign different valences to stories with the same content; and different standards, in which partisans see information favoring the other side as invalid or irrelevant. Their field experiment found that selective categorization did explain the hostile media effect, though they also found some evidence of different standards.[23]

Recent trends

The sociology-of-news perspective might argue that news is news. All journalists are trained to report the news in similar ways, creating a homogenization of news content across news media. With the evolution of traditional media and the emergence of the internet, however, the media landscape is changing rapidly. Chapter 1 noted that the web is much more than just another channel for presenting news content found in other media. The new forms of news and public-affairs material offered on the web reflect its basic characteristics as a unique form of mass communication relative to more traditional forms. Journalists are just beginning to understand the strengths and weaknesses of this new medium and what types of stories can be told effectively within it.

One major change in journalism brought on by the rise of the web has been blogging, although there are ongoing debates as to whether blogs reflect a true form of journalism. Blogs typically offer brief accounts of their author's observations or details they have come across on a given topic, but the degree to which these details have been thoroughly scrutinized for accuracy has raised concerns for many in the journalism profession.

This type of cyber journalism is constantly evolving, and the manner in which stories are told varies greatly from one blog to another. There appears to be a clear emphasis, however, on constantly providing new information through a blog. The various pieces of information may not form a coherent whole like you may find in a *New Yorker* magazine article or a longer package put together by CNN, but blog details do reflect pieces of information collected by an individual and placed in some type of narrative on the web. A key question is whether the processes of information gathering and storytelling for blogs are similar enough to traditional journalism to warrant defining blogging as journalism, or should we define this new type of information gathering and storytelling as something altogether different than journalism? This is more than a quarrel over semantics—this debate centers on the fundamental processes and products that define journalism as a profession.

Since anyone from cooks to Christians can blog, the lines are blurred between journalists and nonjournalists. If a journalist is someone who gathers information, puts the information in an accessible form, and transmits it to the public, this definition certainly describes many bloggers. Of more concern, however, is whether news blogs follow traditional news standards of objectivity and balance. Singer calls this into question, noting that 61 percent of the postings she analyzed contained personal opinion at least occasionally.[24] Williams and Delli Carpini have an even dimmer overview of the internet and politics. They argue that the unlimited information on the internet essentially eliminates the role of the gatekeeper. Because the internet has no gates, there no longer are any gatekeepers providing accurate and fair information to consumers, a pessimistic view with negative implications for public opinion.[25]

Blogs appear to be taking an increasingly important role in public opinion. Because blogs can provide content that is vastly different from the traditional media, they potentially could influence political attitudes much the same way as radio commentators are influencing listeners. Blog readers maintain control over the content that they read—exerting selective exposure, which could ultimately reinforce previously held positions and polarizing political views. When popular blogs focus on a new or neglected issue they can be influential. Journalists at traditional media sometimes find story ideas in blogs. Most readers, though, understand that blogs are not necessarily news. Readers understand that bloggers are often posting their own opinions, so the effect of blogs is not as strong as the effect of news stories.

Blogs come in many different forms, but here we offer three classifications reflecting varying balances of original content versus content created by other individuals or news organizations. There are blogs that offer little to no original content, but instead offer links to a host of bits of news provided by other individuals or organizations. The Drudge Report (http://www.drudgereport.com) is one of the most influential sites in this category. A second type of blog offers more of a balanced mix of original content versus work created by other outlets. *The Huffington Post* (http://www.huffingtonpost.com) is a strong example of this type of web site. *The Huffington Post* will often include reporting by journalists from other news organizations, but will then create original content that feeds off or complements the content from the other sources. A third type of blog offers largely original content that cannot be found elsewhere. *Daily Kos* (http://www.dailykos.com) is a well-known example. This type of blog thrives on providing up-to-date information about what is going on in politics. In addition, blog postings on a site of this kind may come from newsmakers as well as those individuals who are covering the newsmakers. For example, *Daily Kos* has offered postings from former U.S. President Jimmy Carter, current U.S. Senate Majority Leader Harry Reid, and former U.S. Speaker of the House Nancy Pelosi.

Amateurs also are able to create blogs: a web page where the web logger "logs" all the other pages she finds interesting, and sometimes writes original content (often opinion related). And some mainstream media have embraced these types of blogs. MSNBC, for example, tracks blogs through its series "Connected: Coast to Coast," while CNN's *Inside Politics* has a segment it calls "Inside the Blogs." And there are millions of blogs available on the web.

Much of what can be found in the blogosphere relative to news and public affairs content is decidedly more opinion-oriented than what can be found in more traditional outlets like *NBC Nightly News*, *Time*, *The New York Times*, or National Public Radio. Each of the blogs identified above align themselves with specific ideological threads—*The Drudge Report* being more conservative, *The Huffington Post* and *Daily Kos* being decidedly more liberal in orientation. Blogs do not seek the larger mass audiences desired by the more traditional media outlets. Seeking to establish a devoted niche audience, they are much more willing to offer opinion and are less concerned with whom they offend. There are news-oriented blogs which seek to offer their own objective coverage of the major issues of the day, but the blogs that are attracting the most notoriety and devoted audience base seem to be those that offer some measure of opinion reflecting a clearly defined place along the political ideology spectrum.

Other channels for news

Blogs are but one way in which the web is being used in unique ways to create and distribute news content. For example, the British Broadcasting Corporation (BBC) is using Twitter, a free social networking site that allows individuals (in this case, journalists) to post brief text messages (140 characters or less). YouTube is another vehicle for offering news content on the web. YouTube allows individuals or organizations to post streaming video on the web and to categorize it in ways that allow it to be attached to other videos offering similar content. Individuals who wish to engage in the practice of journalism need not wait to be hired by a television news organization in order to create and post a video story for mass consumption. All that is needed is a digital camera (several of which now offer in-camera editing); a computer armed with some basic editing software; and YouTube for the distribution of the content. It is even possible to move directly to distribution via YouTube through the use of a smart phone's abilities to capture moving images and audio. However, it is not just average Joes and Janes who use YouTube as a means to present public-affairs material. Newsmakers also now regularly use YouTube to distribute their message. For example, the 2006 campaign of now-U.S. Senator Jim Webb (D-VA) posted a video clip of his opponent, former Senator George Allen (R), making a series of racially inflammatory remarks to a person who was videotaping Allen at a small campaign event. The video clip became national news and led to Allen losing his Senate seat. In short, just about everyone connected with news and public affairs, citizens and journalists alike, now uses YouTube as another means by which to distribute content.

Public journalism

Some news organizations have sought to increase the involvement of citizens through "public journalism" or "civic journalism." These efforts typically highlight a specific public concern in order to raise local awareness, with the hope that increased awareness will bring about change in the community. Public journalism proponents believe that the news media are obligated to go beyond merely covering events and informing the public with facts and should empower communities to implement changes.

Jay Rosen notes that public journalism is designed to connect citizens with the news media so that the public will become more engaged, interactive, and informed.[26] Arthur Charity describes public journalism in terms of consciousness raising, working through issues with the community, and, ultimately, issue resolution. In this way, the media provide a forum for discussion with the citizens playing a key role.[27]

The basis behind public journalism is different from traditional journalism in one important aspect. Traditional journalists have stayed far removed from civic life, aiming to be detached observers of news events. Public journalism, on the other hand, requires greater involvement from journalists, especially in the identification and presentation of potential solutions to the problems reflected in major news events. Whether public journalism accomplishes its goals has been hotly debated. Frank Denton and Esther Thorson found increased interest and knowledge in politics among those aware of a public journalism project in Madison, Wisconsin.[28] Thorson, Ekaterina Ognianova, James Coyle, and Edmund Lambeth also found that a public journalism project in Missouri had a positive impact on the public's perceptions of the local news media's accuracy, relevance, and competence.[29] There have been, of course, other public journalism projects that failed to achieve their goals.[30]

Regardless, the news media continue to seek ways of getting citizens involved in the news. Some news organizations are highly reliant on citizens for news content. The South Korean online newspaper *OhMyNews!*, for example, has all of its content submitted from citizen reporters. Attempts to replicate this citizen journalism approach in the United States have been less success-ful. The internet, however, offers many opportunities for citizen involvement. Some news media provide forums, chat rooms, and blogs that citizens can use to discuss issues. Thus, while the momentum for public journalism has slowed recently, citizen involvement continues to increase through the internet.

Conclusion

Although many changes are taking place in the media landscape, fundamental questions about the reporting of the news remain highly relevant. Foremost among these are the sources of influence that shape the news reports available to citizens. Key among them are the news routines of journalism, long-established news values, and procedures that define gatekeeping. Journalists' personal backgrounds have far less impact on the topics that they select and how they frame those topics. These gatekeeping decisions also are shaped by the culture of media organizations, the news sources relied upon, and, ultimately, the larger social culture of their community.

Of course, some critics contend that the outcome is a biased news report. Some claim the news media have a liberal bias and favor the Democratic Party. However, an equally vocal group of critics believe the media have a conservative bias favoring the Republican Party. In the half-century since presidential candidate Adlai Stevenson commented that America was a country with a two-party system and a one-party press—in his view a Republican press—there have been dozens and dozens of systematic investiga-tions of bias. On balance, this massive set of evidence indicates a lack of partisan bias in the news. Nonetheless, many people on both sides of the political spectrum perceive a bias in the media, an outcome called the "hostile media effect" in which individu-als perceive the media to be biased against their political views, regardless of whether they are conservative or liberal.

Beyond these basic aspects of news reporting, questions have been raised in recent decades about the adequacy of the information supplied to citizens by the news, and in an increasingly interactive media environment, what role individual citizens should play in the origination and framing of news reports. Proponents of public journalism believe that the scope of the news report must be expanded to facilitate the public discussion of issues at levels beyond the official deliberations of public officials and the pronouncements of politicians. More recently, this has included the active participation of individual citizens in roles formerly the exclusive preserve of professional journalists.

The contemporary debates about public journalism and citizen journalism now take place in the presence of new media channels that are vastly different from the traditional news media. Blogs and Twitter are major new channels for the dissemination of news about public affairs, channels that are instantaneous and make little or no pretense of being balanced or objective. And popular social media such as Facebook add an even more personal dimension to the dissemination of news about public affairs. Understanding the effects of all these perspectives and channels, both traditional and contemporary, is essential to our knowledge of news and public opinion.

3

Trust in the News

Source credibility has long been recognized as a key factor in communication. Aristotle conceptualized source credibility as consisting of three dimensions (character, competence, and goodwill), and these three dimensions remain at the heart of many contemporary research traditions.[1] This important source characteristic is distinct from the content of the message, and there is compelling empirical evidence that recipients' perceptions of the source of a message influence the overall impact of that message.

Journalism and mass communication scholarship has focused for decades on the credibility of news relative to a range of democratic outcomes, and the issue of news credibility has been addressed from a variety of methodological perspectives. Some investigations use survey research to focus on audience perceptions of news credibility while other research has employed experimental methods to study the influence of alternative message structures in producing varied perceptions of news credibility. In addition, there are analyses of the dimensions of news credibility that reflect more of a critical-cultural perspective.[2] Altogether, this collective multi-method approach to news credibility has produced a variety of research findings best described as disparate.

Inconsistent research findings regarding news credibility may be due in large measure to the lack of a clear conceptual definition. Shyam Sundar offers a very succinct definition, "a global evaluation of the objectivity of the story," while Erik Bucy focuses on the concept of "believability" when discussing a message's or news channel's credibility.[3] Overall, the research has tended to focus on the dimensions of "trustworthiness" and "expertise" in defining news credibility.[4] These two dimensions most closely align with the character and competence dimensions of source credibility found in the persuasion literature, while little research attention in news credibility research has been devoted to the goodwill dimension.

Mattias Kohring and Jörg Matthes designed a multidimensional scale of trust in news media, a concept they equate with news media credibility.[5] Trust in news media is conceptualized as a single higher-order construct consisting of four lower-order dimensions: selectivity of topics, selectivity of facts, accuracy of depictions, and journalistic assessment. Others also have noted that it is important to distinguish among several levels of analysis when discussing the issue of news credibility. Wolfgang Schweiger identified six different source levels: the presenter (e.g., TV news anchor), the source/actor (e.g., politician), the editorial unit (e.g., specific newspaper article), the specific media product (e.g., CBS Evening News), subsystem of media type (e.g., public television), and media type (e.g., newspapers).[6] Five of these six levels pertain directly to the news as source, with only the source-actor level referring to someone/something being covered by the news. These distinctions are important because one level nested inside another level does not automatically equate to a one-to-one transfer of audience perceptions of credibility. For example, an audience member may not think highly of Brian Williams (i.e., presenter), but feel NBC News (i.e., media product) on the whole is a quality news organization that produces a credible product. At the same time, this person could also hold a very low opinion of broadcast TV news (i.e., media type) as a means by which to gain any understanding of the world, but still think highly of NBC News, which is nested within the medium. News credibility needs to be understood at each level, and there is solid evidence showing considerable variation in how people perceive different reporters, news organizations, and media forms.

This chapter will examine credibility from two perspectives. First, attention will be given to the role of credibility relative to different journalism models. Three models will be examined: the market model, the advocacy model, and the trustee model. Discussion will then turn to the present high level of interest in news credibility. What do people think of the news they are receiving? All lines of social science research go through cycles of low versus high interest within the academy, and the study of news credibility can claim a resurgence of interest in recent years. This is due largely to three elements. One is the rise of the web as a new and ever-evolving source for public-affairs information. Another is the creation of public-affairs outlets that target their attention and criticism on "the liberal media" and make a concerted effort to raise public doubt about the credibility of traditional news organizations. The third is the increased popularity of political comedy outlets that satirize traditional news, such as *The Onion* and *The Daily Show with Jon Stewart*.

Journalism models and news credibility

There are three distinct models for the role of journalism within a larger social system.[7] First, there is the market model. This model takes a "give the people what they want" approach to mass media in general and journalistic content in particular. With rising concentration of media ownership, many have argued that this has led to news organizations being run by businesspeople, not journalists. Indeed, it appears that news organizations are increasingly bowing to market concerns, especially profitability, in terms of content creation and distribution. The Project for Excellence in Journalism's 2007 annual report reported that an increasing number of journalists, both national and local, find their profession to be on the wrong track. Bottom-line business interests driving news content was mentioned prevalently among disaffected journalists.

As for the role of news credibility and the building of a news audience within this journalism model, it can cut both ways depending on what you think of the audience and its desire for certain types of news content. If you believe audience members by and large desire credible news coverage, then a market approach would lead to news organizations seeking to generate a highly credible product. If you believe that most audience members do not care about the credibility of their news content, then journalistic norms created to generate credible content will be of little value relative to market demands. Both scenarios are correct to some degree. The percentage of the mass audience who truly desire a highly credible news product in their daily lives may be fairly small. However, news credibility may be extremely important for the subpopulation of audience members who can best be defined as *news junkies*.[8] This much smaller group may find true value in credible news information and make media consumption decisions according to where they feel they can find highly credible news. If most citizens would forego the consumption of news content altogether when given a full range of media options, however, then credibility as a defining characteristic of news content would suffer within the market model. News credibility may not be a dimension of media content that the vast majority of citizens think about when making media-use decisions, either choosing within a range of news media outlets or across a wider range of entertainment versus news media options.

The second model is the advocacy model, best reflected by the partisan press that defined American journalism until the rise of the Progressive era. As Kaplan noted, "Throughout the nineteenth century, American journalism was publicly and forthrightly partisan."[9] The dominant newsroom perspective for a very long period of time was one defined by political partisanship. Within this model, "journalists were not antagonists of politicians, but appendages . . . The press's authority to narrate American social reality derived from its affiliation with a party."[10] While the advocacy model may have been on the decline within American journalism for much of the twentieth century, other countries have retained a relatively stronger advocacy model to the present day, especially within specific media forms. For example, Patterson found that Italian and German print and broadcast outlets were much more likely to retain a strong advocacy model than their American peer outlets.[11] In addition, British print and Swedish broadcast outlets were also rated higher in terms of advocacy versus neutrality. In short, there is wide variation in the current state of the advocacy model in different national media systems.

Audience perceptions of news credibility become highly fractured within the advocacy model. The objectives of a partisan press are not to be balanced or fair. Instead, credibility is purely perceptual. A news outlet gains credibility among certain subpopulations based largely on its implicit or explicit association with a political party, while simultaneously losing credibility among other subpopulations who are members of opposing political parties. Credibility can be generated by a news organization through a political party affiliation, but it is not a form of credibility that is meant to appeal to all citizens, nor is it a form of credibility that can be defined by criteria reflective of fairness or balance. Trust in the information may still exist for some, but that trust stems from a belief that what is offered in the news report is the stance of the party, not from some inherent sense of the information being accurate.

The last of the three approaches to journalism is the trustee model. Michael Schudson has stated that the trustee model is defined by "its commitment to reporting over commentary . . . [and] an ideology of objectivity, professional codes of ethics, and principles of disinterested public service."[12] Ideally, journalists working within this model "consider themselves devoted . . . to the service of truth alone."[13] Credibility of news is obtained in this model through the ideal of neutrality, freedom from "the ubiquitous contention of the public sphere," and the use of the scientific method for purposes of information gathering.[14]

Unlike the advocacy model, where news credibility is almost purely perceptual and frequently defined by political party associations, news credibility in the trustee model can be objectively defined based on some universal criteria, and stems in large measure from the news outlet *not* being affiliated with a political party. Credibility as defined by the trustee model best fits current social scientific explications of this concept, that is, it incorporates fairness, balance, objectivity, truthfulness. In terms of the audience, the issue of whether a particular reporter, news organization, or medium is credible may be largely perceptual, but within the trustee model normative ideals have been established which can be used to look at the relationship between these objective measures and audience perceptions.

In short, the value and role of an objective assessment of news credibility varies widely based on the type of journalistic model, and it may be best to think along a continuum ranging from the advocacy model on the left, to the market model in the middle, to the trustee model on the right. Any objective assessment of news credibility is inconsequential under the advocacy model. Credibility is based purely on partisan perceptions, and a news organization will be deemed credible by a certain subpopulation of the electorate if it is affiliated with a particular point of view. Under the market model, there can most certainly be an objective assessment of news credibility, but within this model perceptions of news credibility will be of interest to only a small segment of the citizenry, such as news junkies or elites. The objective assessment of news credibility is of greatest interest under the trustee model where the credibility of news information is pertinent to all members of the citizenry, not just the few.

Contemporary perceptions of credibility

Ongoing research by the Pew Center for the People and the Press about the American audience's perceptions of news credibility does not paint a healthy picture. Their surveys have reported declines from the mid-1990s into the new century in perceptions of credibility. Even in the 1990s, most news media could claim only around 30 percent of the American population believing "all or most" of the information being offered by that particular news organization. By 2006, no news outlet could claim that level of credibility. For major daily newspapers, the percentages of the American population in the "all or most" category were *The New York Times* (20 percent), *Wall Street Journal* (26 percent), and *USA Today* (18 percent). The picture is equally dire for television. All three major networks (NBC, CBS, and ABC) could claim only 22 percent of the people believing "all or most" of what was offered on their broadcasts.

There are similar declines for local news. The 2007 State of the News Media Report by the Project for Excellence in Journalism notes that local TV news declined from 34 percent in 1985 to 22 percent in 2006 of the survey respondents stating that they found this information source "highly believable." Local daily newspapers fell to an all-time low with just 23 percent of the American public finding these sources "highly believable." There is good news in a recent report by the Donald W. Reynolds Journalism Institute, however, which found that audience members who consume local news through a local news media website find these websites to be highly credible, giving it a mean score of 5.60 on a 7-point scale.

Both the present state and the decline in news credibility among the American media audience needs to be qualified by political party identification. The news credibility gaps between Democrats and Republicans are staggering. For example, the 2006 Pew survey revealed that 32 percent of Democrats believed "all or most" of what *The Lehrer Newshour* on PBS reports, while only 13 percent of Republicans fell into this same category. A similar credibility gap was found for a wide variety of other news organizations. Only two organizations were ranked higher by Republicans relative to Democrats—Fox News and the *Wall Street Journal*.

It is important to recognize that the influence of political party identification on perceptions of news credibility may not be showing a direct effect. There clearly is a possible role for political party identification as a moderator of the trends in news credibility over time. If we focus on the decade of the mid-1990s through to the mid-2000s, we need to assess whether Republicans were in a steeper decline in terms of perceptions of news credibility. This is one example of the importance of stepping beyond simple main effects in analyses of what influences perceptions of news credibility.

Personal characteristics also need to be addressed when looking at perceptions of news credibility, and these individual differences need to be addressed within the context of the type of news being presented. For example, Christopher Beaudoin and Esther Thorson found race—black versus white—to be a significant predictor of news credibility.[15] Their study of audience perceptions of three Minneapolis-based news organizations revealed the black audience to perceive lower levels of credibility when the news organizations were covering blacks, whereas the black audience perceived these news organizations to be more credible when covering white-related issues.

How do audiences of non-Western news media outlets view these outlets in terms of their credibility? Thomas Johnson and Shahira Fahmy recently surveyed Al-Jazeera audience members, nearly all of whom were from Arab or Muslim countries.[16] Al-Jazeera audience members rated this news source very high in terms of believability, accuracy, trustworthiness, and expertise. All the means were above 4.0 on 5-point scale. This Arab news source was rated far higher in each of these categories when compared to the BBC, CNN, and local Arab media. Interestingly, local Arab media were rated the lowest in each category by the audience members. These data point to the lack of an Arab bias in the sample that would translate into high credibility ratings for all Arab-based news media outlets. Instead, it is only Al-Jazeera that can claim a privileged position in the survey. These results are backed up by Ali Jamal and Srinivas Melkote, who found that Kuwaiti viewers of Al-Jazeera turned to that news media outlet due to the lack of credibility of Kuwaiti government-run news organizations in that country.[17]

Influence of credibility on news media use

The concept of news credibility is especially important because perceptions of news credibility predict news consumption. It is important to note, however, that the relationship between news credibility and news consumption needs to be carefully considered in terms of how both concepts are defined. Wayne Wanta and Yu-Wei Hu found that the believability of a news medium has only small, nonsignificant correlations with exposure to that same news medium.[18] Believability is highly correlated with reliance on the medium, however.[19] In turn, reliance is significantly related with exposure. Thus, news outlet believability has an *indirect* effect on news outlet exposure through the mediator of reliance.

Spiro Kiousis employed a broader definition of news credibility that included perceived factuality, belief that the medium was driven more by profit than public service, privacy invasion, community concern, and level of trust.[20] The relationships between these measures and media exposure were found to be statistically significant, albeit weak, for newspapers and the web. However, the correlation for television hovered around zero. In short, there are decidedly weak correlations between news credibility and news use, with the most consistent effect of news credibility on news exposure coming in the form of indirect effects.

The web as a news source

Overall, online news outlets are more or less on par with more traditional news outlets when it comes to perceptions of news credibility. Andrew Flanagin and Miriam Metzger found online news to be rated relatively equal with broadcast media sources like television and radio, but ranking lower than newspapers.[21] Similarly, Kiousis found online news to rank slightly higher than traditional television news in terms of audience credibility ratings, but slightly lower than daily newspapers. Schweiger found similar results in Germany, with newspapers ranking higher than online news and online news remaining relatively equal with television news in terms of overall credibility.[22] In short, online news does not stand out as being inherently more credible in the eyes of audience members, and it is clear that some traditional media forms, particularly newspapers, rank higher in credibility when directly compared to online news. However, it is also important to note that *nontraditional* internet information sources are seen as particularly weak in terms of perceived credibility.[23]

It also is essential to assess potential moderator variables that may influence the news credibility ratings of online news. For example, Bucy found age affected perceptions of news credibility ratings.[24] He collected two samples, one consisting of traditional college students and the other a standard adult population. The student sample rated online news as more credible than the adult sample using a five-item credibility index based on ratings of fairness, accuracy, believability, informative, and in-depth coverage. When this index was disaggregated, however, he found the primary age differences were in perceptions of how informative the web was and the level of in-depth coverage found on the web. Younger adults ranked the web much higher on both criteria compared to the ratings found in the older sample. Bucy also found that the younger sample found traditional media forms such as television news to be more credible than the web, while the older group rated the web more credible than traditional television news.

Sundar found identical patterns in how people think about the credibility of online news and traditional news sources.[25] The four broad factors to emerge from Sundar's 21–item measure for traditional news media were credibility, liking, quality, and representativeness. The credibility factor consisted of three dimensions: biased, fair, and objective. The same four factors were found in the online news measures, and the same three dimensions were associated with the credibility dimension.

A slightly different picture emerged in another investigation of online news credibility where there was a trustworthiness factor, a currency factor, and a bias factor.[26] The bias factor may be due in part to survey respondents rating web-based news sources as more biased than newspaper or television news sources. Although there may be slight variations in how audience members conceive of online news credibility relative to more traditional news media outlets, there are many more commonalities than dissimilarities between old and new media in this regard.

Examination of online news credibility needs to be continuously updated due to the changing nature by which online news sources, even those sites affiliated with traditional news organiza-

tions such as *The New York Times Online* and washingtonpost.
com are offering public-affairs content to citizens. For example,
the day following American presidential candidate Senator Hillary
Clinton's Democratic primary win in West Virginia on May 13,
2008, washingtonpost.com offered a traditional text story with
the following headline, "Clinton's rout in W. Va. might not be
enough." Connected to this article was a "comments" hyperlink
where users could offer a comment on the article or the subject
matter of the article, or provide some random bit of information that may not have been directly connected to the article or
the subject matter. One audience member offered the following
post:

> The one point I disagree with you on though is where you said
> McCain is in the shadows and irrelevant. The problem with this is, the
> media have yet to put him on the carpet for a whole slew of issues and
> the fight between HRC and Obama isn't helping that matter. McCain
> has gotten a HUGE pass from the media to this point and that really
> disgusts me.

The "you" reference in this post is for the washingtonpost.com
article. This audience member is providing direct commentary on
the points raised in the washingtonpost.com article. How might
these types of comments influence general perceptions of the credibility of the more traditional political campaign coverage offered
by washingtonpost.com? How do the two types of content work
together to influence the broader credibility of washingtonpost.
com? These empirical questions are important for understanding
news credibility in a digital age.

Use of audience feedback alongside the presentation of original news content has been a source of great debate among media
professionals.[27] One true innovator of the technique has been
huffingtonpost.com, which takes existing news media content
from other sources, reworks that content to fit its purposes, provides space for audience commentary, as well as offering "highly
opinionated posts of an apparently endless army of both celebrity
. . . and non-celebrity bloggers."[28] The rise of this type of web
site speaks to a possible return to more of an advocacy model of

journalism on the web rather than retaining the trustee model as the standard. The major difference between the digital age and the advocacy model of bygone generations is that the advocacy outlets are not now directly tied to a specific political party.

An additional question about online news organizations concerns who the news organizations decide to partner with in their presentation of public-affairs material. As previously noted, washingtonpost.com for a time partnered with the satirical news outlet *The Onion*. One can find on washingtonpost.com links to fake satirical news articles at the bottom of traditional news articles written by washingtonpost.com reporters. Why would washingtonpost.com partner with a fake news organization like *The Onion* in terms of the issue of organizational credibility? In terms of character—trust—as well as competence—expertise, *The Onion* articles should do nothing but reduce the credibility of washingtonpost.com. However, attaching washingtonpost.com to *The Onion* for purposes of branding washingtonpost.com may be very positive for the news organization from the standpoint of the goodwill dimension of source credibility. The goodwill dimension is defined as the "intent toward receiver" as perceived by the audience member.[29]

James McCroskey and Jason Neven point to three goodwill dimensions: understanding, empathy, and responsiveness. It is the understanding dimension that appears to best reflect the rationale behind the partnering of news with fake news. The understanding dimension reflects the degree to which the receiver of a message believes the source of the message "gets the point."[30] The newspaper site washingtonpost.com is showing its readership that it gets the point that they like to consume both traditional news and satirical news. The site is showing that its own approach to the news is exactly the same as that of their audience. McCroskey and Neven argue that "goodwill . . . has become the lost dimension of ethos/credibility" that needs to be explored with the rise of online news.[31]

In terms of the responsiveness dimension of a source's perceived goodwill, this could be reinforced by offering audience comments alongside traditional news content. Responsiveness is defined as "one person acknowledging another person's communicative attempts."[32] What better way for a news organization to demonstrate communicative responsiveness than to supply audience comments alongside their news content? Traditional media outlets can offer only a very limited version of communicative responsiveness, such as letters to the editor in newspapers or reading letters on a news talk radio show, and there is always the lingering sense that the traditional media's responsiveness is heavily edited. Online news organizations allow audience member comments to be posted that are filled with outlandish claims, misspellings, as well as insightful, reasoned arguments/commentary. Once again, the credibility of online news may have much more to do with goodwill than trust or expertise.

Rise of the advocacy model

The HuffPost—huffingtonpost.com—is a well-known example of the rise of the advocacy journalism model on the web. The rise of the advocacy model can be found in traditional media outlets as well, and is particularly evident on talk radio and cable television.[33] The strengths and weaknesses of the advocacy model versus other journalism models is part of the discussion of credibility, but the rise of Fox News as a public-affairs advocacy outlet is of particular interest to the discussion of news credibility, given some of its dominant message themes.

It is clear that Fox News has established itself as an identifiable brand whose principal dimensions are a conservative political ideology and dynamism.[34] Content analyses of specific programs on Fox News such as *The O'Reilly Factor* reveal that the dynamism comes from a clear adversarial tone,[35] whereas the conservatism comes from who and what are the focuses of the channel's adversarial messages—the "liberal" media, the political left, foreigners, and the intellectual elite. It is the "liberal" media adversary that is of particular interest to our discussion of news credibility. The influence of outlets such as Fox News, which constantly states the need for audience members to distrust traditional news outlets, may be particularly corrosive when looking at the state of news credibility ratings in America. Not only can the advocacy model serve to change the role of credibility in the functioning of journalism in society, but outlets that choose to attack traditional news media also may be able to create a sense that the old concept of news credibility, the trustee model, is deeply flawed and should simply be discarded altogether.

There is little question that Fox News is attracting audience members who already think poorly of the press, and this is true for politically conservative talk-radio programs such as Rush Limbaugh as well. The empirical question left unanswered, however, concerns the extent to which this selective exposure to politically conservative public-affairs outlets that constantly state negative perceptions of traditional news credibility strengthens or further reinforces pre-existing attitudes as a set of reinforcing spirals.[36] Another important question is the degree to which these reinforcing spirals shape use of traditional news media over time. Bennett found that there is little relationship between conservative political talk-radio use and consumption of more two-sided traditional news media outlets like the daily newspaper or the national nightly broadcast TV news.[37] Do these reinforcing spirals generate a *reduction* in traditional news use over time, however?

Satirizing the news

The Daily Show with Jon Stewart offers its audience a satirical view of not only the major stories of the day but the journalistic tasks of information-gathering and storytelling as well. The program offers Stewart an opportunity to provide comedic interpretations on a wide range of public-affairs topics. As Geoffrey Baym has argued, "The show functions as *both* entertainment *and* news, simultaneously pop culture and public affairs."[38] This cable television show devoted to political and journalistic satire is unique for American television, but the show's format stems from previous comedic outlets using a similar mode of presentation as a vehicle for social commentary: for example, *Saturday Night Live*'s Weekend Update.

All forms of satire, whether they are political or some form of broader social commentary, have been defined as "pre-generic,"[39] in that it is in the nature of satire to exploit pre-existing genres. In the case of *The Daily Show*, the pre-existing genre is the national television newscast, and the basic aesthetics of the program, such as the opening music and studio setting, mock TV newscasts. In this sense, *The Daily Show* is like other forms of satire in that it is "a playfully critical distortion of the familiar."[40] Audience members, no matter the degree to which they regularly watch national television newscasts, have at least a limited understanding of the genre's format. *The Daily Show* uses the audience's familiarity with these newscasts as a means by which to satirize the practice of journalism.

The Daily Show averages more than a million TV viewers for its original airings, and consumption of *The Daily Show* clips on the web is vigorous. The program points its satirical poker not just at those individuals and social institutions making headlines, but also at the news industry that constructs the headlines. A recent content analysis completed by the Pew Research Center notes, "The press itself is another significant focus on *The Daily Show*. In all, segments about the press and news media accounted for 8 percent of the program time." The press/media ranked as the fifth most often discussed topic on *The Daily Show* in 2007, while this same topic did not even make the top 10 most often discussed topics in the mainstream news media.

The potential negative effects of *The Daily Show* on basic democratic processes have been the source of much debate, and there is some empirical evidence pointing to negative effects on perceptions of traditional news outlets. One experiment found that viewing *The Daily Show* prior to viewing *CNN Headline News* resulted in audience members thinking less of traditional news in terms of being able to provide political information gratification.[41] This experiment also found that the effect was moderated by internal political self-efficacy, however. Specifically, the influence of *The Daily Show* on perceptions of traditional news media was found only among those individuals who were low in political self-efficacy. The influence of the satirical program was nonexistent for those individuals high in self-efficacy. In short, those individuals who were already more inclined to be disengaged from the political process embraced the message of *The Daily Show* that traditional news media cannot be trusted. Conversely, those individuals who were high in self-efficacy walked away from viewing *The Daily Show* thinking the same of traditional news as those individuals in the control condition. When there is an influence on audience perceptions of traditional news media, a key question is whether the types of attitudes being produced reflect a healthy skepticism of news or a true disrespect for the profession and the role of journalism in society.

Conclusion

This chapter has focused on the concept of credibility and why it is essential to understand the degree to which citizens trust their news outlets when analyzing the relationships between news, public opinion, and a host of democratic outcomes. There also is a need to understand that news media credibility takes on different definitions and roles depending on the dominant journalistic model of the times.

The rise of alternative "news" outlets such as Fox News, which privately discard the trustee model of journalism (while trying to embrace it publicly) and which seek to raise credibility concerns about its competitors, could make people think less of journalism. Another form of media that is important in this regard is the increasingly popular satirical news outlets such as *The Daily Show with Jon Stewart* and *The Onion*. Not only is there explicit content offered in these outlets that finds fault with traditional journalistic practices, but the formats of these outlets present an implied message to audience members that one should find traditional news highly questionable. Researchers have only begun to address how the use of these media outlets functions alongside the consumption of traditional news, much less how the complementary relationships formed among these multiple types of media use influence political knowledge, attitudes, and behaviors. Added to this mix is the ever-changing variety of channels and content available on the web.

II

Setting the Civic Stage

4

The Audiences for News

The news media are working though a profound era of change. Shifting demographics, the rise of new media and communication technologies, and new types of competition have created an uncertain time for journalism. This chapter begins with the most basic concepts in mass communication: audience, media exposure, media attention, and media use. It is essential to gain an understanding of these core concepts and the distinctions among them, especially given that there remain wide variations in how these concepts are described theoretically and operationally.

The chapter will then focus on some broader patterns of use among the public for various news outlets. Chapter 1, A Changing Communication Environment, offered details on the current level of use for a range of traditional sources for news—newspapers, newsmagazines, broadcast television—and emerging outlets that are becoming more prominent within the news media landscape—online sources. Moving beyond basic audience levels for news media across different types of outlets, this chapter will focus on the broader patterns of news consumption that are creating clear distinctions between different subpopulations.

It is important to gain an understanding of how individuals' use of various news media work in coordination with one another as we begin to think about how news has an impact on a wide variety of democratic outcomes. The focus of this particular discussion will be on how one type of media use serves to complement other types of media use. In addition, an argument will be made about the need to abandon the idea that the various news media are in competition with one another for the attention of the news audience. One unequivocal empirical fact is that most members of the audience engage multiple information outlets in order to remain up-to-date on public affairs at the international, national, regional, and local levels. It is necessary to understand these relationships among different types of media use.

Defining the audience

Webster argued that there are three core metaphors used to organize our thoughts about the audience as a theoretical concept: audience as mass, audience as agent, and audience as outcome.[1] Each metaphor represents a limited way in which to approach the concept of audience, and attached to each metaphor is a central question that embodies the metaphor.

For the audience as mass, the central question is "What media do people consume?" This approach to the audience focuses squarely on patterns of media consumption, but little to no attention is given to *why* people are consuming one form of communication versus another, or making one specific program choice within a medium versus another content choice within that same medium. The metaphor of audience as agent better addresses the notion of why different people choose to consume various media. Its central question is "What do people do with media?" Finally, the metaphor of audience as outcome focuses on the consequences of media consumption, and its central question is "What do media do to people?" The primary focus of this chapter will be on the first of these three metaphors, audience as mass, while the other two metaphors will be covered in more detail in subsequent chapters.

It is important to recognize that "audiences are not natural things. They are *man-made*."[2] The audience-as-mass approach views the news audience as a commodity that can be bought or sold based on the nature of the media content being offered. An audience forms around some central focus of attention, and the focus of this chapter is on what audiences exist for the different types of news that are being offered across the media landscape. The types of news vary across a range of dimensions, such as breadth, depth, or ideology, and a different mix of content dimensions will result in the construction of a different type of audience. In addition, the audience for a particular news item depends on a host of structural features related directly with the issue of access. For example, broadcast television news has an inherently larger audience than cable television news.

The goal of this chapter is to offer a baseline idea of the size of various audiences for different outlets and different types of news material within specific forms of mass communication. In order to do this, we need a clear sense of how to measure an audience, and for this we need a basic understanding of the core concepts of media exposure, media attention, and media use.

Exposure, attention, and use

People often fall into the habit of using the terms "exposure," "attention," and "use" interchangeably. These concepts have very different meanings, however. Exposure serves as the baseline measure of the news audience. Without exposure there can be no attention, but that does not mean that there is a perfect correlation between the two. News exposure refers to just coming into contact with a specific news outlet or some type of content within that outlet. The typical question asked in surveys of the news audience asks individuals how many days in the past week they have come into contact with a specific news outlet—for example, reading a daily newspaper or viewing broadcast television news.

Simple exposure needs to be contrasted with the concept of attention, which is defined by Steven Chaffee and Joan Schleuder as "increased mental effort."[3] Someone may be exposed to a TV news broadcast each evening, but this consistent level of exposure does not automatically translate into an equal and consistent level of attention to this news. Perhaps this person is a single parent who had to spend time with their child two of the nights in the past week helping with homework while the news was on, or a meal was being prepared—the primary activity—while the TV news was playing in the background—the secondary activity. For the remaining nights the TV news may have captured the fuller attention of this individual, but it is clear from these scenarios that the level of attention was far more inconsistent across the week than was basic exposure.

As Chaffee and Schleuder have argued, "Measurement of attention in addition to simple exposure more adequately reflects the person's use of television news."[4] Exposure and attention to any type of news each offer a unique causal influence on a series of democratic outcomes, but it is the combination of the two items that serves to reflect best the concept of media use.

In turn, there are significant concerns about how to measure media exposure, attention, and use. Markus Prior has found that traditional self-reports of news media exposure are riddled with overestimates.[5] People will commonly report being exposed to far more news than their actual levels of exposure. While the most typical motivations, such as social desirability, were found to play little to no role in generating overestimations, Prior did find that poor memory and tainted inference rules were the most likely culprits in generating biased individual-level estimates. Prior has argued that one way to reduce the overreporting of news media exposure is to ask individuals to compare themselves with others so that an anchor can be placed within the question posed to a survey respondent. This approach to the measurement of media exposure does not alleviate the problem in full, however.

Comparing different types of media exposure and attention measures, Anca Romantan, Robert Hornick, Vincent Price, Joseph Cappella, and K. Viswanath found the traditional measure of media exposure to be a poor predictor of an individual's knowledge.[6] Their best measures were open-ended queries that are not particularly practical. On another front, Chul-Joo Lee, Robert Hornick, and Michael Hennessey argued that it is important to recognize the high levels of measurement error that often exist in these measures, and the strength of specific media effects may be prone to attenuation if this measurement error is not properly accounted for.[7]

Broader patterns of news consumption

Chapter 1 noted a widening gap between the amount of news consumed by "news junkies," who make up about 10 to 15 percent of the American population, versus other citizens. We will explore this trend a bit further in the current chapter as well as other broader shifts in news consumption and what these shifts may mean for the future of journalism. Increased isolation of "news junkies" from the rest of the citizenry relative to overall levels of news consumption is just one form of audience segregation. Several other forms of audience segregation also need to be explored, such as segregation on the basis of demographics, particularly age, sex, and race. In addition, attention will be given to politically oriented individual differences, such as party identification and ideology.

The rise of cable television with several hundred content options and the web with its seemingly infinite number of content options has presented those individuals who are true, hardcore news consumers a feast that can last 24 hours a day, seven days a week, and 365 days a year. There have always been news junkies, but the news has never been so readily available and in such a steady stream.

One initially might think that such broad bandwidth would be eagerly welcomed by news organizations but there is another side to the story. Cable and the web have brought, as well as news, a multitude of entertainment-based options for media consumers, and it is clear that the general audience for news in the face of all these entertainment options is growing ever smaller. The contemporary news audience is more dedicated in terms of its level of consumption, but news no longer reaches the wide swath of the media audience it enjoyed in the past. It is easy in today's media environment to navigate through numerous content options without ever coming into contact with what would be classically defined as news, whereas this was not the case even 10 years ago.

In short, there will always be a market for news. There is a segment of society that finds tremendous value in having access to quality information about the major issues of the day. The last decade, however, has seen developments concerning who makes up the news audience and the actual size of this audience. The news audience is much smaller now than in years past as a percentage of the general population. But this does not mean that the core news audience is not diverse in its tastes for different types of news and unique media forms. There are some clear choices that different subpopulations are making in terms of what types of news to consume.

Segmentation by age

Younger generations turning away from news, shifting their media consumption habits to non-news outlets, entertainment-based "fake news" outlets, and alternative forms of mediated entertainment, such as video gaming, have been much discussed. But Dannagal Young and Russell Tisinger found that audience members who watch programs such as *The Daily Show with Jon Stewart* also consume a fair amount of news.[8] In short, there does not appear to be a great deal of time displacement when it comes to entertainment-based public affairs stepping in to replace traditional news consumption. Instead, they serve as complements of each other, and this is especially true for younger news consumers. Although it is clear that the audience for programs such as *The Daily Show* and *The Colbert Report* are younger than the traditional news audience, this does not mean that those who watch these sources of political satire do not also consume traditional news.

This makes sense from the standpoint of uses and gratifications. Only those audience members who have a solid handle on the news of the day will find true gratification in the content being offered in the satirical representations of the news. News use functions in part as a necessary but not sufficient condition for the consumption of political humor. If someone did not have a firm grasp of the latest issues concerning the wars we are waging, the economic policies being implemented by the government, or other major issues, that person's amusement at Jon Stewart or Stephen Colbert would be extremely limited. One of the most politically knowledgeable audiences in media is *The Daily Show* audience. This is most likely not due to the wealth of political information Jon Stewart is supplying. The most likely reason for the high level of political knowledge among the *Daily Show* audience is that one needs to be knowledgeable about politics in order to be able to understand the political satire.

Where we do see a segmentation of news consumption by age is with regard to different media forms. Particularly worrisome is the rising median age of the typical consumer of traditional news outlets. Younger news consumers are simply not following in the footsteps of their parents and grandparents in making the daily newspaper or the evening network TV newscast part of their daily routines. The young demographic has begun to turn to new media in larger numbers in order to gain an understanding of what is going on in the world and in their communities.

This does not mean that one form of media use is completely taking the place of another type of media use. It is particularly important to understand how the use of old media functions in coordination with the use of new media. The thrust of the empirical evidence we have to date speaks of only a minority of audience members giving up old media wholesale for new media.[9] Nevertheless, it is clear that it tends to be the young who are gravitating to new media. In short, there is a clear case to be made for age segmentation in news consumption via traditional media outlets versus new media outlets. The single best demographic predictor of newspaper use, broadcast television news use, and online news use is age, with a clear positive association being found in the first two cases and a clear negative association being evident in the last of these three relationships. We should not react by treating old and new media as being in competition with each other. There is clear evidence that people do consume one in coordination with the other in order to gain a more well-rounded sense of the major issues of the day, but the overall patterns of which type of outlet dominates these media-to-media relationships will vary according to the age of the media consumer. Those individuals in the younger cohorts will use online sources as their dominant outlets, while individuals in the older cohorts will use more traditional media outlets as their base for news.

Segmentation by gender

Gender has always been a consistent predictor of traditional news use, but it does not have the same predictive strength as other demographic variables such as age. Men are slightly more inclined to consume the traditional sources of hard news—the daily newspaper, broadcast TV news, and newsmagazines—as compared to women. The opposite appears to be the case for soft news. The audience for this type of programming tends to be dominated more by women than by men. Soft news includes programming such as *Entertainment Tonight*, but Baum has shown that a tremendous amount of public affairs information can be found within these programming options. In addition, use of these nontraditional news outlets has been shown to influence political attitudes. Thus there appears to be a small but important gender gap when it comes to the type of news being consumed by men versus women. This is an important distinction because the nature of the storytelling taking place in hard news versus soft news is quite distinct for such issues as the military and international conflicts.

Building on the theme of various news outlets not being in competition with one another, Baum argues that soft news can serve as a gateway to the consumption of hard news.[10] Soft news consumers may learn about political and public policy matters incidentally through the consumption of soft news, but they may then seek out additional hard news content on these topics, once they have been exposed to matters that affect them personally or that strike their interest. Feldman and Young found that those who watch a great deal of late-night comedy shows showed an increased interest in and consumption of traditional news over the course of the 2004 U.S. presidential primary season.[11] As with online versus traditional news, it is important to step back from treating soft news and hard news in isolation. The use of one influences the use of the other, and any discussion of media effects must take these relationships into account.

Segmentation by ethnicity

The State of the News Media Report 2008 provides a detailed assessment of the rise of ethnic news media outlets across the United States. For Latino communities, the real growth area for Spanish-language news media is not the large, urban metropolitan areas. There has been a clear lack of growth since 2000 for Spanish-language newspapers in these areas. Instead, the areas for potential growth are the smaller communities that have seen a recent surge in new immigration. The primary targets for this type of news outlet are those individuals who are recent arrivals to the country, not those generations that have become part of the mainstream culture.

This report also points to Asian-American news media having a large upside in their potential for growth, noting that there has been a 300 percent increase in Asian-American media outlets from 1990 to 2007. Every expectation is for the number of these outlets to grow for years to come, given the uptick in immigration from Asia. In television news, we have seen the launching of New Tang Dynasty Television, a 24/7 news channel that reports the news in several Chinese dialects and is directed solely at an Asian-American audience.

African-American news media have been a part of major American metropolitan areas for many decades. A listing of major African-American daily newspapers would include the *Jackson* (Mississippi) *Advocate, Los Angeles Sentinel, New England Informer, New York Beacon*, and the *New Journal and Guide* (Virginia) to name just a few. While African-American–based television channels such as BET do have a news component, most topics covered are soft news rather than hard news. However, 2010 will see the launching of the Black Television News Channel

(BTNC), the first 24/7 news channel devoted to reaching out to an African-American audience. Finally, the 2008 American presidential campaign and the election of Barack Obama as the United States' first African-American president brought witness to the importance of radio as a source of news and information for African-American communities. This is not surprising, because radio attracts an African-American audience that is highly educated, has substantial household income, and is more likely to vote than the national average.

The rise of new media outlets seeking to serve different ethnic communities speaks to a segmenting of the news audience along ethnic lines, at least to some degree. There are few data on how much crossover exists between the consumption of ethnic news media and mainstream news media, but it is clear that ethnic-based news media will continue to be on the rise as the nature of the American population continues to change in terms of ethnicity. Some argue that ethnic-based news media provide a valuable service by dealing squarely with issues of primary importance to specific ethnic groups, a focus that simply can't be provided by mainstream news media. Critics of these news media organizations argue that the rise of ethnic-based news media and the reporting of news in languages other than English can create further barriers to assimilation. We do not wish to take a stand within this particular political debate, but we can state with some certainty that ethnic-based news media will continue to be a part of the media landscape for some time to come. In fact, its share of the news audience most likely will continue to grow.

Relationships among news media

Citizens use multiple news media outlets to survey the world around them and discover what major events and issues may affect them. However, there has been far more attention to how people use particular news media and less attention to how the use of various types of news media are related to one another.

In the benchmark 1940 Erie County study, Lazarsfeld and his

colleagues did find a substantial overlap in people's use of the various mass media. Comparing exposure to newspapers, radio and magazines, the primary media of that time, they concluded:

> People highly exposed to one medium of communication also tend to be highly exposed to other media. There are relatively few who are highly exposed to one medium and little exposed to the other.[12]

More recently, McLeod, Scheufele, and Moy demonstrated that reading a daily newspaper was positively related to the use of other traditional news information sources like television news.[13] And Shah and Scheufele outlined a model where television news use led to an increase in newspaper use, and newspaper use was found to have a direct effect on the consumption of web news.[14] Looking at media effects, Holbert outlined a process of media influence where presidential debate viewing was a mediator of the relationship between TV news use and strength of vote choice, the key relationship in this case being television news as a strong, positive predictor of presidential debate viewing.[15]

More generally, Holbert and Benoit argue that specific types of news media use continue to predict other types of news media use across time.[16] In addition, Holbert and Benoit qualify Chaffee's basic adage that "communication breeds more communication" to argue that communication breeds more like-sided communication. Zaller argues for a distinction between one-sided and two-sided information flows,[17] and Holbert and Benoit equate these to the advocacy and trustee models of journalism. Use of news outlets that embody more of the trustee model of journalism—that is, they offer multiple sides to a story—predicted the subsequent use of other types of news embodying this same approach to reporting the major issues of the day. For example, use of newspapers and traditional nightly national television news were predictors of themselves across time. In addition, newspaper use was found to be a positive predictor of subsequent television news use and vice versa. These relationships found between what are predominately two-sided outlets reflect the trustee model of journalism. Reflecting the advocacy model, relationships also were found between use of the one-sided, advocacy-oriented news outlet of Fox News and the use of conservative political talk radio.

In addition, there is evidence that using almost any form of political campaign media predicts presidential debate viewing. Both one-sided and two-sided news media use are positive predictors of subsequent debate viewing. The use of ideologically driven one-sided outlets such as Fox News, however, and two-sided outlets such as broadcast television, tend to have little or no relationship with one another. In short, there is a distinction between those citizens who use ideologically driven media outlets and those citizens who use outlets that tend to offer multiple sides to public-affairs topics. Prior has argued, however, that the audience for an ideologically driven television news outlet such as Fox News is not wholly distinct from the audience for a more two-sided TV outlet such as CNN.[18] There is a significant percentage of television news viewers who use both of these cable TV news providers.

Conclusion

This discussion of the news audience—in reality, many audiences—has identified important distinctions among news media exposure, news media attention, and news media use. The news media audience also is segmenting along multiple lines, and this chapter has outlined several key fissures relative to different types of news. All these fissures reflect the different ways in which news organizations are abandoning attempts to reach a truly mass audience and are moving to isolate specific subpopulations from which a base audience can be formed in order to sustain profitability.

Age was discussed in relation to old versus new media, and relative to the rise of what has come to be defined as satirical "fake news." Gender was considered: males have a greater proclivity for hard news, while women tend to be dominant in the soft news audience. There is also the rise of ethnicity-based news media and the segmenting of the news audience along racial lines. Finally, the advocacy model of journalism appears to be on the rise, along with segregation of the news audience along political party and ideological divisions. Each of these forms of segmentation can create new stress points for a democratic society.

Reporters who gather information and put together a coherent narrative about a topic deemed worthy of news coverage are storytellers. And storytellers have power in that the stories we hear allow us to gain a sense of connection with others in our society, to establish a shared value system, and to build a sense of social capital. Increased segmentation of the news audience, however, means that not all of us are receiving the same set of stories. For example, consider the presentation of the 2008 American presidential election. There are clear distinctions in the way this election, and the major players taking part in the election, were presented in traditional news versus fake news, in hard news versus soft news, in ethnic-based versus traditional news outlets, and on advocacy-oriented blogs versus trustee-oriented traditional media.

If we as citizens are not receiving the same stories about the major issues of the day, then there will be a disconnect in how we approach these topics. This is not an argument for needing a singular form of news coverage within our democratic society. It is only in totalitarian regimes that this would be possible, and the notion of mandating the way all reporters should cover a given story goes against our basic democratic ideals. We must also recognize, however, what may be lost when the news audience becomes so segmented that it does not receive stories that share at least some commonality. Perhaps there is a golden mean that allows a democracy to function well, and we are left to constantly seek out that mean, that balance. Nonetheless, this chapter has outlined how the news media audience is both shrinking and becoming increasingly segmented. Both of these developments have potentially profound effects on our democracy.

Finally, there is the need to better understand how use of multiple news outlets works in coordination to produce civic outcomes. The most fruitful way to examine news media exposure, attention, and use is to consider multiple forms of news use simultaneously. No one type of media activity functions in isolation from other types of media engagement by an audience member. There is a need to step away from treating various forms of news media use as being in competition with one another, and to adopt the perspective of looking at complementary relationships.

5

Focusing Public Attention

Interest in the role mass media play in the political process, particularly in the area of persuasion, stretches far back into the last century, when the earliest days of empirical communication research were tightly focused on exploring the dynamics of attitude change. Typically, these inquiries investigated opinion and attitude change within the confines of controlled experiments and sample surveys.[1] Subsequently, due to minimal success in locating dramatic swings in audiences' attitudes, a limited-effects model of media influence emerged, a view that the impact of mass communication was minimal and operated through a litany of mediating forces.[2] Of course, a major reason for these conclusions was the singular focus on attitudinal outcomes rather than the broader focus on outcomes that define the hierarchy of media effects extending from simple awareness to behavioral outcomes.

In response to the premise of limited media effects, research began probing other domains of human experience where mass media influence might be evident, and the cognitive revolution in the social sciences led to the same approach in mass-communication research. As a result, there was a shift to examining the cognitive impacts of mass media, and it was in this realm that news media influence was found to be highly consequential. In what has become known as the agenda-setting function of mass communication, one major consequence of news coverage was the determination of which issues were most important in public opinion; news media thus shaped the topics of discourse in public affairs. As succinctly summarized by Cohen, the press may not be successful much of the time in telling people what to think, but it is stunningly successful in telling its readers *what to think about*.[3] This relationship is the center of attention in this chapter, which traces the genesis of agenda-setting theory, the contingent conditions of the agenda-setting influence of the news media, and the contemporary expansion of agenda-setting into new settings and domains.

Origins of agenda-setting theory

In their landmark study of undecided voters in Chapel Hill, North Carolina, during the 1968 U.S. presidential election, McCombs and Shaw examined the extent to which news media attention to political issues corresponded with what voters subsequently thought was the most important problem facing the nation.[4] Their expectation was that the issues covered by mass media would increase the salience of those issues in public opinion. To test their hypothesis, they completed a content analysis of nine news outlets and surveyed 100 undecided voters in the local community. Comparison of the pattern of news coverage with voters' views on what were the most important issues of the day yielded strong support for this hypothesis.

It is also noteworthy that these relationships with a wide variety of news media were stronger than what would have been predicted based on the platform of key issues presented by the political parties during the election. Thus, this evidence dismissed the possibility that selective exposure and retention processes could be alternative explanations for agenda-setting effects rather than news media. In the earlier research that had found only minimal media effects, selective exposure and retention processes were frequently cited as the explanation for minimal changes in attitudes and opinions.

Though the Chapel Hill study provided correlational evidence for the effects of issue salience in news coverage, the investigation was not specifically designed to explore whether a causal relationship existed between news content and public opinion. So a follow-up analysis was conducted in Charlotte, North Carolina, during the 1972 U.S. presidential election. By monitoring both the news and public opinion over time, Shaw and McCombs were able to scrutinize the sequence of influence more directly.[5] Their panel study of a random sample of registered voters found evidence that shifts in news media attention toward political issues preceded similar changes in public opinion, lending support to the notion that the agenda of issues highlighted in news media influenced the agenda of issues in public opinion.

While the panel design of the Charlotte study was considered more rigorous for examining causal relationships, most scholars assert that experimental verification is required to conclusively assert causal linkages among variables. A series of experiments by Shanto Iyengar and his associates in the 1980s addressed these questions in a controlled setting.[6] Using television newscasts, these researchers artificially emphasized certain political issues in broadcasts shown to participants in order to ascertain whether this increased emphasis would affect these issues' perceived importance. Consistent with previous research, they found compelling support for the proposition that the news media played a principal role in influencing which issues are perceived as important among citizens. A related finding, germane to understanding the persuasive consequences of news, was that by shifting issue priorities in individuals' perceptions, the news media also swayed the standards by which political leaders are evaluated, a process called priming that will be discussed in detail in Chapter 7.[7]

Over time, more complex longitudinal research studies have been employed to test the agenda-setting role of news media. One of the earliest and most important empirical investigations of agenda-setting, however, also used longitudinal data. G. Ray Funkhouser examined news magazine content and public opinion about the Vietnam War, race relations, campus unrest, inflation, crime, drugs, and poverty.[8] His results revealed media influence on issue priorities among the public for key concerns across the decade of the 1960s. Of particular significance was the finding that not only did public opinion follow trends in mass communication content, it did not follow real-world trends associated with these issues, thereby accentuating the pronounced role of mass communication in molding collective perceptions.

A subsequent examination of articles in *The New York Times* and public opinion concerning the civil rights issue detected robust agenda-setting effects over a 23-year period and suggested that the optimal time lag for issue salience effects to emerge from news coverage is four to six weeks,[9] though the time lag has fluctuated in other studies. The time-lag question is central for understanding the appropriate span of time in which to observe the relationship between news coverage and public opinion. Another inquiry probing linkages between economic headlines and public perceptions of the economy across 13 years also confirmed agenda-setting effects.[10] Finally, MacKuen and Coombs collected longitudinal evidence of agenda-setting impacts for domestic and foreign policy issues during the 1960s and 1970s, demonstrating associations across many different types of issues.[11]

A *variety of evidence*

The Acapulco typology—named after the location of the conference where it was first introduced—is useful for understanding this diverse evidence about agenda-setting. According to the typology, which is outlined in Figure 1, studies can be grouped along two dimensions. The first distinguishes between those inquiries examining a set of issues or only a single issue. The second distinguishes between those measuring the public agenda at the aggregate level or the individual level. As a consequence, the literature can be divided into four basic classifications:

- Type 1: Mass Persuasion, with its focus on a set of issues with aggregate measures of the public agenda, for example, the Chapel Hill study,
- Type II: Automaton, with its focus on a set of issues with individual measures of the public agenda, which is discussed below,

- Type III: Natural History, with its focus on a single issue with aggregate measures of the public agenda, for example, the 23-year civil rights study, and
- Type IV: Cognitive Portrait, with its focus on a single issue with individual measures of the public agenda, for example, the experimental studies by Iyengar and his associates.

Over the years since Chapel Hill, extensive empirical support has been found for three of the categories, but limited corroboration has surfaced for the Automaton model (Type II), which asserts that news media attention to a set of issues would stimulate higher levels of perceived salience for those exact same issues at the individual level. This, of course, would assume a highly passive audience that simply is manipulated by shifts in media emphasis, an assumption not supported by empirical data.

	Measure of Public Salience	
	Aggregate data	Individual data
Focus of attention		
Entire agenda	Perspective I	Perspective II
	Mass Persuasion	*Automaton*
Single item on agenda	Perspective III	Perspective IV
	Natural History	*Cognitive Portrait*

Figure I: The Acapulco Typology: Four Perspectives on Agenda-Setting

In total, over 400 studies have investigated agenda-setting dynamics in a wide variety of contexts and settings, including many in Europe, Asia, and South America. One investigation

comparing the United States and Britain reported a positive relationship between the salience of foreign affairs in news media and
public opinion in both nations.[12] An earlier investigation comparing agenda-setting relationships between television and print news
for public issues in West Germany found more robust associations
for exposure to newspapers, but did observe some connections
with television news as well.[13] A similar conclusion was reached
for a study of Japanese mayoral elections in 1986.[14] Evidence from
Argentine elections in 1997 indicated considerable voter learning
from the news media agenda between the beginning and end of the
election campaign.[15] Finding agenda-setting effects in countries
outside of the United States is largely dependent on the extent to
which these countries have open governments and media systems.

Beyond aggregate-level research, inquiries at the individual level
measuring attention to news and the perceived public salience
of issues also have shown agenda-setting impacts, though they
are substantially smaller in number by comparison. Nonetheless,
general media exposure has been positively connected to increases
in the public salience of political issues. Illustrating this is a
unique study of a mainly Hispanic sample in McAllen, Texas,
which found that audience attention to Spanish-language media
predicted shifts in perceived issue importance, but attention to
English-language media did not.[16]

One explanation for the widespread evidence of agenda-setting
influence is the relative uniformity of topics in media content. The
issues that the news media tend to cover are similar across a wide
variety of print, broadcast, and online contexts. The concept of
intermedia agenda-setting suggests that elite media outlets such
as *The New York Times* serve as a guide or proxy for other news
organizations regarding the major issues of the day. Gatekeeping
research on the interactions between journalists and their sources
further verifies this pattern. As a result, tracking audience attention to a specific news outlet is not necessary in order to observe
the agenda-setting outcomes of issue salience in news coverage.

Beyond consistency of the topics on the media agenda, the way
in which media salience is conceptualized and measured sheds
further light on how the news shapes public opinion. The most

common approach for measuring media salience is by attention. From this perspective, salience is akin to media awareness of an object, usually gauged by the sheer volume of stories or space dedicated to various topics in newspapers, television news, and so on. Another aspect of media salience is prominence, which refers to the position of a story within a media text—something that communicates its importance.

Contingent conditions

Despite the widespread evidence for agenda-setting, this is not a universal news media effect. Several contingent conditions have been identified that affect the magnitude of this news media impact. For example, the distinction between obtrusive issues—those with which citizens have direct experience—and unobtrusive issues—those with which citizens have little or no direct experience—is critical with regard to media influence on public perceptions of issue priorities.[17] Mass media influence is greatest for unobtrusive issues. In particular, public concern about foreign policy matters, such as wars, mirrors news media attention to a greater degree than domestic matters, such as the economy, because of the direct experience individuals have with many domestic issues.

A related constraint on agenda-setting impact involves the small number of issues that can be salient in public opinion at any one time. Agenda-setting dynamics operate as a zero-sum game, meaning that an increase in the salience of one issue on the public agenda translates into another one declining or being removed. At the same time, the diversity and range of issues on the public agenda has grown over time, a trend largely attributed to the increased education level of the American public during the last century. Nevertheless, the average number of issues on the public agenda at any one point in time is around three or four.

In addition to the nature of the issues, audience characteristics affect the scope of agenda-setting relationships. The concept of need for orientation offers a psychological explanation for the magnitude of agenda-setting effects. According to this perspective, individual differences in the desire for orienting information explain differences in attention to the media agenda, and differences in the degree to which individuals accept the media agenda. Conceptually, an individual's need for orientation is defined in terms of two lower-order concepts, *relevance* and *uncertainty*. Relevance is the initial necessary condition. Individuals have little or no need for orientation in situations with low relevance. Among individuals who perceive the relevance of a topic to be high, additional consideration of their level of uncertainly distinguishes moderate and high levels of need for orientation. Under conditions of high relevance and low uncertainty, the need for orientation is moderate. When both relevance and uncertainty are high, need for orientation is high. The greater an individual's need for orientation, the more likely they are to reflect the media agenda.[18]

This approach to understanding the psychological dynamics behind agenda-setting presupposes that audiences are active processors of information. An alternative view is that issue priorities are changed through a short-term, essentially automatic process because news media make certain issues more accessible in individuals' minds, thereby boosting their salience. However, two recent experiments failed to find any support for the hypothesis that accessibility mediates the relationship between media exposure and agenda-setting effects.[19]

Demographic differences among individuals, such as age, income, and education, play only minor roles in enhancing or minimizing the impact of news media on public perceptions of issues. Across three different age groups in Louisiana, Coleman and McCombs found that the basic agenda-setting relationship was robust despite different levels of exposure to traditional and new media among the generations.[20] The gap between the issue priorities of different demographic groups also closes when comparing heavy news consumers versus those who pay minimal attention to public affairs.[21] Using data comparing a nationwide sample based on gender, race, and education, Du found that agreement among perceptions of issue importance rose as media attention among different groups climbed.[22] A central outcome of mass media attention for public opinion is to help create consensus about what issues are most salient among disparate groups in society.

With a trend of increased fragmentation and diversity in news media outlets, the question of whether there are major differences among the communication channels carrying news becomes more significant. Over the years, research has scrutinized differences among agenda-setting effects for print and broadcast channels, as well as mounting attention directed toward the internet in recent years. The evidence shows mixed results concerning differences based on channel characteristics. For example, the original Chapel Hill study of agenda setting found stronger relationships for newspapers. A subsequent study during the 1976 U.S. presidential election, however, found support for greater influence from television news.[23] An investigation of the 2000 presidential campaign showed agenda-setting relationships with public opinion for television, newspapers, and candidate web sites.[24] Television news appears to have more immediate effects on public opinion, but the duration of effects via print media are longer. With the ongoing changes in the media landscape, this is likely to remain a lively topic.

Beyond issue salience

Although the main focus of the media's agenda-setting effects historically has been on issue salience, the media's role in affecting salience goes beyond political issues. In explaining this idea, McCombs submitted that in the abstract agenda-setting is about the transfer of salient elements from one agenda to another.

> When the key term of this theoretical metaphor, the agenda, is considered in totally abstract terms, the potential for expanding beyond an agenda of issues becomes clear. In most discussions of the agenda-setting role of mass media the unit of analysis on each agenda is an object, a public issue. However, public issues are not the only objects that can be analyzed from an agenda-setting perspective.[25]

The idea of agenda setting can be used to understand the role of news in shaping the prominence of a multitude of topics in the news. For example, news media exert influence by increasing the perceived visibility and importance of political candidates during a political campaign. When thinking about the presidential primary process, especially in the early phases, it can be argued that news media determine to a considerable degree the "agenda" of viable candidates from which voters will select. This is a powerful influence on voters' decisions at the ballot box. On an even broader level, every four years news media attention stimulates the salience of politics itself in society as citizens normally not engaged in public affairs become involved to learn about issues and candidates in preparation to vote in national, statewide, and local elections.

Extending agenda-setting beyond politics, research on business news has found that news media attention contributes to the salience of corporate reputations and product perceptions among consumers, employees, and investors. Charles Fombrun and Mark Shanley also found that general media attention toward 292 U.S. companies was negatively tied to *Fortune* magazine's annual reputation ratings.[26]

In the international arena, news media are a critical force in shaping the perceptions of foreign nations in public opinion. The extent to which citizens are concerned with and have cognitions about a foreign country is primarily driven by media coverage. One comparison of national television news content and public opinion revealed that increased coverage of foreign nations was associated with higher levels of public concern about those countries.[27] Exemplifying this point in a contemporary context, public opinion polls showed marked increases in public concern with Iraq, Iran, and North Korea after President George W. Bush's famous State of the Union Address in 2002 identifying this group as an "Axis of Evil."

Attribute agenda-setting

In addition to influencing topic salience, the explication of a second level of agenda setting has linked the concept with framing by suggesting that news media attention also can influence *how* people think about a topic by selecting and placing emphasis on certain *attributes* and ignoring others. Elaborating on this theoretical development, McCombs and Salma Ghanem state:

> Just as objects vary in salience, so do the attributes of each object. When journalists and, subsequently, members of the public think about and talk about various objects, some attributes have center stage. Others are relegated to lesser roles, and many are absent altogether. Just as there are agendas of objects, there also is an agenda of attributes for each object that can be organized according to the relative salience of the attributes.[28]

This emerging area of news media effects has frequently examined political candidate images. Specifically, if the news emphasizes a politician's experience, then public descriptions of that candidate also will stress that characteristic. While the relationship between second-level agenda setting and framing has been widely debated, Hsiang Iris Chyi and McCombs declare that "thinking of frames as attributes of an object provides the theoretical link between agenda-setting and framing research."[29]

Attributes have both substantive and affective elements. Substantive attributes deal with aspects of messages that help us to cognitively structure various topics. Some examples of substantive attributes in candidate images are ideology and issue positions, qualifications, biographical information, and integrity. For issues, substantive attributes include sub-areas—for example, unemployment and economic stimulus programs as sub-areas of the economic problem, as well as such aspects of the issue as proposed solutions and problem definition frames in communication messages. In contrast, affective elements deal with the positive, neutral, or negative tone present in communication messages. These affective elements will be considered in greater detail in Chapter 8.

To empirically explore second-level agenda-setting effects, Guy Golan and Wayne Wanta studied attribute salience processes during the 2000 New Hampshire primaries. Their study involved three newspapers and public opinion among voters.[30] Their findings demonstrated that the agenda of candidate attributes highlighted by the newspapers corresponded closely with the agenda of attributes among voters. An investigation of the 1996 Spanish general election found similar patterns for both television and newspaper content.[31]

Support for attribute agenda-setting effects also has been gleaned for a variety of issues in the news. Mark Benton and P. Jean Frazier's analysis of media coverage regarding economic sub-issues and the perceptions of Minneapolis residents in 1975 offered corroboration for issue attribute effects associated with newspapers, but not television news.[32] More recently, an investigation of news coverage and the public salience of the attributes of terrorism among residents of Columbia, Missouri, found modest second-level agenda-setting effects.[33]

In a synthesis of both levels of agenda setting, the media salience of attributes also can contribute to the salience of objects among members of the public, an idea known as the "compelling-arguments" hypothesis. One investigation of presidential candidate images over five elections found that perceived candidate salience was positively related to media coverage of moral quality, but only moderately connected to coverage for intellectual ability.[34] Variations in how topics and persons are portrayed in the news, and the consequences of these attribute agendas in the media for public opinion, are central to our understanding of media effects.

Conclusion

One of the major cognitive influences of news media is to focus public opinion on particular objects and attributes in the news. Collectively, the evidence obtained for first- and second-level agenda-setting effects of the news media on public opinion has been very robust over a wide variety of settings historically, geographically, and substantively. Ironically, the proposition that media shape what we think about and how we think about it takes us back to the role of news media in shaping attitudes, opinions, and behaviors, a journey that once again returns us to the seminal question considered by Lazarsfeld and colleagues regarding the impacts of mass communication. This journey continues in Chapter 7, but first Chapter 6 will examine what people learn from the news, the step that is intermediate in the hierarchy of media effects between awareness and the formation of attitudes and opinions.

6

Learning from the News

Knowledgeable citizens are essential to an efficiently functioning democracy. And of course, the news media are important sources of information, readily available to citizens. This acquisition of knowledge is a transactional model. Reporters gather information and transmit it through some communication medium. Individuals receive this information and mentally process it, with the result that much of what individuals know about public affairs is based on the information provided to them by the media. In detail, however, the process is much more complex. Individuals do not receive all the information transmitted by the media. Some individuals learn more efficiently than others. And exactly what do individuals know?

Knowledge and memory have been examined in many ways, and one of the key distinctions in the nature of an individual's knowledge of public affairs is between recognition and recall. *Recognition* involves whether individuals can correctly identify something they have been exposed to previously. Visual communication provides many examples of recognition. For instance, persons may be exposed to several photographs of a news event. Later, these same persons will be shown a series of photographs and asked if they recognize any of the photographs from the first set. There are two ways, of course, that their responses could be incorrect. They might falsely identify a photo that was not in the first set, or they might fail to identify a photo that was in the first set.

Recognition can also be examined with verbal questions. You could ask someone: "Which of the following is the Supreme Court Chief Justice?" The answer categories would then be read, one of which would be the correct answer, John Roberts. In other words, recognition essentially involves multiple-choice questions, similar to those asked on a university exam.

In contrast to recognition is *recall*. Here, respondents are asked questions in which they must provide the information from memory. The answer categories are not given. For example, "Who is the Chief Justice of the Supreme Court?" These are similar to "fill in the blank" questions.

Broadly, *recognition* deals with a comparison of the information presented with one's memory, while *recall* involves a search of memory first, then a comparison after the information is located. Usually, individuals are far more efficient at recognition than at recall.

Barriers to knowledge acquisition

While the news media provide considerable amounts of information about the news of the day, several factors can act as barriers, inhibiting efficient reception and learning by individuals.

First, individuals may experience interference. With multiple potential sources for information, content from one source could conflict with other sources. An individual may be exposed to a news story that says the city council is discussing a budget that would provide little or no increase in spending. This same individual may have had a discussion with a co-worker criticizing the city council for large increases in spending.

Another potential barrier to learning is memory decay. Psychologists as far back as the nineteenth century found extremely rapid decay in individuals' memory. There is far more evidence supporting interference than memory decay in inhibiting learning, however. Complicating knowledge acquisition is the fact that many media messages have two main types of information: verbal and visual, which sometimes conflict. Research suggests that learning visual information is easier for most people than learning verbal information. Doris Graber examined recall of verbal and visual information in television news and found memory for visual information was more than double that for verbal information.[1] She concluded that accompanying visuals were one factor contributing to the effectiveness of individuals at retaining stories and retrieving them from memory. Raymond Nickerson conducted a classic study in which he showed participants 600 photographs on various topics. The participants were able to recognize 92 percent of the visual information after one day. After one year, they were still able to recognize 63 percent of the visuals.[2]

Measuring knowledge

A vast array of measures has been used to tap into the knowledge levels of individuals. These have included questions that were open-ended and closed, that involved recognition and recall, and that dealt with general and domain-specific topics.

Some surveys simply have asked respondents how knowledgeable they believe they are about certain topics. Asking respondents about the level of knowledge they have on a subject does not necessarily measure knowledge; instead it measures perceived knowledge. Suppose that I am asked: "How knowledgeable are you about brain surgery?" I might answer that I am an "expert" on brain surgery. I certainly know this involves a surgical procedure in the cranial area that is often done to remove tumors in the brain. I probably know enough about brain surgery that I could write a paragraph for Wikipedia. If I were asked to conduct a brain surgery procedure, however, I would have no idea how to proceed. Expertise about something may well not equal expertise in something. The language of self-reported knowledge can be extremely inexact, and open to much interpretation. The original question that sought to determine a respondent's level of knowledge about brain surgery leaves too much room for individual interpretation. A respondent's idea of knowledge may not meet the intent of the person posing the question. And the answer of one respondent is not necessarily a valid comparison with another person's reported level of knowledge.

Closed knowledge questions sometimes ask respondents about factual information and provide multiple-choice response categories. These types of questions can produce inaccuracies as well, as questions and response categories can give clues to the correct answers. Multiple-choice questions on college tests have received a great deal of criticism for being inaccurate measures of student learning.

A different way to measure knowledge is to ask respondents an open-ended question involving factual information. Two problems often arise from these questions. First, researchers must consider how precise a response needs to be before it is judged accurate. Suppose a survey asked how many deaths are attributed to second-hand smoke each year in the United States. The American Lung Association estimates this number to be 50,000. If a respondent replied 60,000, would that mean that he/she has no knowledge of second-hand smoke? What if the respondents said 100,000 or 500,000?

Second, factual information is not necessarily how we learn. Many people would know that second-hand smoke is a killer, and that many people die each year from second-hand smoke. On the other hand, few people would be able to come up with the exact number of deaths as reported by the American Lung Association. The precise number is not relevant to most people. But the fact that thousands of people die each year is information that people would deem important enough to store in their memories.

Finally, there are unaided recall questions that essentially ask a respondent, "Tell me everything you know" about a specific topic. The respondents then can talk as much or as little as they desire. Researchers subsequently content-analyze the responses, looking for key terms that demonstrate a certain level of knowledge of the respondent. These unaided recall questions often are coded on an interval level scale, depending on the number of key words a respondent mentions.

As with the other types of knowledge questions, unaided recall also can be problematic. By asking a question such as "Tell me everything you know about . . ." a survey may tap into personality traits rather than knowledge. "Tell me everything you know about the healthcare system in the U.S." might elicit a lengthy list of information from a respondent who likes to talk a lot. A brain surgeon answering the same question might simply say "It is inefficient." Thus, a surgeon with a reserved personality may score lower on knowledge of the U.S. health care system than a person with far less knowledge but a talkative nature.

In addition to the type of questions employed, researchers also have examined different types of information sought. Michael Delli Carpini and Scott Keeter identified two categories: general questions—which include those similar to a high-school civics exam, such as the Congressional vote margin needed to overturn a presidential veto—or domain-specific questions—those dealing with facts from recent news coverage, such as the trends in crime rates.[3] General questions are often negatively correlated with age. Younger people can recall civics lessons from high school better than older individuals. Nonetheless, general measures are used frequently because they are widely available. Domain-specific questions, on the other hand, can better tap into knowledge gained from the news media. But these questions tap into individuals' memory for facts and often do not access whether respondents understand the significance of the facts.

Differential knowledge acquisition

Despite the vast amount of information that is increasingly available, there are indications that U.S. citizens are no better informed than in the past. The internet and 24-hour cable television news programming may provide opportunities for individuals to access endless amounts of political information. Nonetheless, voting turnout, with the exception of the 2008 U.S. presidential election, has not increased, and research has consistently found differential learning patterns across individuals. Why are some people more knowledgeable than others?

One reason is the difference in their patterns of media consumption. The news medium a person relies on plays a role in the amount of information acquired. Typically, newspaper readers have more political knowledge than television news viewers. This finding can be attributed to the type of information processing required for the two media. Reading newspapers involves an active process. The act of reading implies that the reader is purposefully paying attention to the content. Watching television, on the other hand, can be a passive process. Viewers can pay little attention to the content if they so desire. And attention to the news is a stronger predictor of knowledge acquisition and media effects than mere exposure.

Motivation for media use also is an important factor. For example, an individual with a strong need for orientation—the psychological concept discussed in Chapter 5—will demonstrate stronger attention to media messages and thus learn more information. A person with a strong need for entertainment may watch *The Daily Show with Jon Stewart* and gain some incidental learning, but the amount of knowledge acquired, while larger than for non-media users, will be less than a purposeful news user.

There are also sources of information that supplement or interfere with media content. For example, political advertising has a strong influence on learning about candidate issues stands and candidate images.[4] Political advertising, of course, allows candidates to elucidate their issues stands without reporters filtering the message. Negative political advertising also can draw significant attention. Voters, generally, do not like attack ads, but nonetheless find them memorable. Whether this increased memory leads to votes is unclear. There is evidence that the attack ads lead to the polarization of the voters, and at times they may suppress voter turnout.[5]

Although the availability of information does not necessarily translate into increased knowledge, the internet does offer hope for the future. In the 2008 election, individuals using the internet for news—about 40 percent of the electorate—passed the percentage of individuals using newspapers for news—about 35 percent. As more people use the internet, new media will play an increasingly significant role in the diffusion of political information.

Gaps in knowledge

Differential learning patterns exist in society. Some people learn a great deal from information in the media while others learn little. These differential learning patterns spawned the Knowledge Gap hypothesis. The basic argument for the existence of a knowledge gap is that more highly educated individuals tend to learn faster and more efficiently than individuals with less education. Philip Tichenor, George Donohue, and Clarice Olien note:

> As the infusion of mass media information into a social system increases, segments of the population with higher socioeconomic status tend to acquire this information at a faster rate than the lower status segments, so that the gap in knowledge between these segments tends to increase rather than decrease.[6]

Several factors contribute to the increased gap in knowledge between persons with low and high socioeconomic status (SES):

- Differences in communication skills
- Differences in the amount of stored information
- Differences in social contact with knowledgeable people
- People with low SES may not find information concerning public affairs or science news compatible with their values or attitudes and, in turn, may demonstrate higher levels of selective exposure and retention for most political news
- Mass media are generally geared toward people of high SES with the result that low SES may have difficulty understanding the news.
- People with high education levels have well-developed learning habits.

Altogether Kasisomayajula Viswanath and John Finnegan identified 13 factors that influence the knowledge gap.[7] Motivation plays a very key role in whether the gap widens or narrows. For instance, if there is a perceived conflict on a local issue, the knowledge gap is likely to decline because the conflict makes the news content relevant to both high and low SES persons.

Models of political learning

To gain an overview of knowledge acquisition, scholars have constructed detailed learning models. Among the most highly researched approaches is the Elaboration Likelihood Model.[8] The ELM was originally used to examine attitude formation, but has evolved to include cognitions as well. This model posits that individuals have two routes for learning: a central route, which requires a great deal of thought, and a peripheral route, which involves a much lower level of thought. Motivation and learning abilities influence which route an individual takes in a particular situation. If an individual is highly motivated to learn and has the available cognitive resources, this person will use the central route. This would imply that a highly complex and informative message would be processed more efficiently. If a person has little interest in the topic and has distractions or time constraints, this person would use the peripheral route, implying that a simple message would be most effective. Additional factors such as source credibility would be more important for messages processed by the central route. The use of a highly credible source, however, could also be used as a "heuristic shortcut"—leading a person to think that experts are always correct—and thus leading to effectiveness in peripheral processing as well.

Adding to the complexity of ELM is that the level of motivation for learning about political news can vary greatly across individuals. In the *Economic Theory of Democracy*, Anthony Downs argues that citizens have little incentive to engage in complex analysis because each person has only a single vote.[9] Thus, for many potential voters, complex political ads with a great deal of information are not processed efficiently because individuals process the ads through the peripheral route.

Michael Schudson, on the other hand, coined the term "monitorial citizen" to describe the manner in which citizens gather information in an age where abundant information exists.[10] He argues that most individuals monitor or scan the news rather than reading it closely. Using this strategy, they can be alerted to problems regarding a wide variety of issues. On the one hand, monitorial citizens are better informed on an array of issues than citizens in the past. On the other hand, however, monitorial citizens tend to be defensive and reactive rather than proactive.

Samuel Popkin makes a similar argument, noting that citizens rely on common everyday events to make political decisions.[11] These events serve as a shortcut for potential voters. This leads individuals to ask questions about whether a candidate would perform well as president that are based on their knowledge of previous events. In other words, low-information rationality draws on information shortcuts and rules of thumb. Popkin concludes that voting is simply making a choice, not explicating a complex situation.

William Eveland's cognitive mediation model takes a different approach.[12] Information processing serves as a mediating variable in the relationship between motivations and political knowledge. Eveland argues that the effects of exposure and attention on knowledge are affected by factors related to information processing: the intensity of involvement with the news, the types of motivation and involvement, and cognitive and emotional involvement. His model posits a causal process that begins with the motivations to learn. These motivations lead to the processing and elaboration of information found in the news, which ultimately leads to knowledge acquisition.

Finally, researchers have borrowed from the psychological literature to examine *schemas,* which are cognitive structures that people use to organize their knowledge and to provide a framework for future learning. Schemas help an individual process information by forming ties to previously held related knowledge. The activation of a particular schema can influence how information is processed and stored. In other words, an observation could take on vastly different meanings depending on the activated schema.

A schema can be activated by explicit thought about its topic or by an encounter with relevant information. Activation is all-or-none; that is, making the schema active renders readily accessible all the structured knowledge contained therein. Even when a schema is below the threshold for activation, it can have a variable level of accessibility, which is influenced by recent or frequent use. A higher degree of accessibility means that the schema can more readily be activated and used.[13]

Conclusion

An informed electorate is the basis of a democratic society. Decades of research examining how individuals learn from mass media messages have added much to our knowledge of this vitally important area. This research points to a complex process in which both message variables and individual factors have key roles in the acquisition of political knowledge.

Motivation is a consistent factor in knowledge acquisition, though whether the causal influence is direct or indirect is the subject of some debate. Education also creates uneven knowledge gains. Individuals with high levels of education typically learn from the media at a faster rate than individuals with low education levels.

A consistent finding is that newspaper readers learn more than television viewers. With the increased reliance on the internet, this could be a double-edged sword. On the one hand, the print versions of newspapers continue to lose readership. On the other hand, internet versions of newspapers are flourishing. With greater opportunities for individuals to gain access to political information, be it from the internet or 24-hour cable newscasts, the potential is considerable for a well-informed citizenry.

7

Forming Opinions

Despite the substantial evidence about the cognitive influence of the mass media on public opinion, the role of news in shaping the opinions and attitudes of citizens in democracy has remained a primary concern throughout the history of mass communication scholarship. Indeed, much of the seminal work in the field was focused on this very question, a question that remains prominent today.

This chapter will trace the influence of the news media in the traditional realm of public opinion: citizens' positive and negative feelings about specific public issues, political figures, and other elements of public life. We will explore the role of news media in shaping, reinforcing, and changing opinions and attitudes about a wide variety of topics. Although this overview is not exhaustive, it does represent a cross-section of the major perspectives on the relationship between news media and public attitudes. Our discussion will first review the classical perspectives on that relationship, followed by an examination of contemporary views, and will conclude with an analysis of the normative implications of the interplay between these forces.

Historical origins

Among the earliest studies exploring the role of news in molding citizen opinions and attitudes were the extensive surveys conducted by Paul Lazarsfeld and his colleagues in Erie County, Ohio, during the 1940 U.S. presidential election and in Elmira, New York, during the 1948 U.S. presidential election.[1] At the outset, there were major expectations regarding the effects of the news media on public opinion, particularly in their ability to prompt attitude change and conversion among voters. In popular circles, a belief existed that the influence of news media on public attitudes was direct and that audiences were highly vulnerable to mass media messages.

Although no formal theoretical framework existed asserting such a simplistic relationship, scholars have retroactively dubbed this viewpoint the "hypodermic needle" model of mass communication. And to some extent, the Lazarsfeld studies did test propositions based on such a conceptual model, probing the impact of radio and newspaper use on voter preferences during these presidential elections.

Contrary to their expectations, they found that interpersonal communication exerted more influence on altering voter preferences (defined as conversion from one candidate to another) than mass communication, and they concluded that the role of the news media was one of reinforcement rather than change. Lazarsfeld, Bernard Berelson, and Hazel Gaudet declared that

> political communications served the important purpose of preserving prior decisions instead of initiating new decisions. It kept the partisans "in line" by reassuring them in their vote decision; it reduced defections from the ranks. It had the effect of *reinforcing* the original vote decision.[2]

Collectively, these findings resulted in the two-step flow model of communication. From this perspective, the impact of mass media on general public attitudes is indirect because exposure to news is thought primarily to sway the preferences of "opinion leaders" (such as family members and friends), who in turn modify the preferences of the general public. Based partially on the theorizing of the two-step flow model, Joseph Klapper argued for a "limited effects" model of mass communication, a perspective that greatly altered scholarly perspectives in the 1960s and 1970s concerning media effects.[3] Despite its widespread influence, the two-step flow model has received substantial criticism over the years as empirical research has mapped situations where the mass media have direct impact on individuals' attitudes and opinions. In addition, there are numerous scenarios where the paths of influence involve multiple steps.

Even the original Erie County and Elmira findings can be viewed as evidence for persuasive effects by the news media. For example, it is critical to note that *opinion change* is just one type of persuasive result that might be attributed to news media exposure and attention. Indeed, the influence on *opinion formation* and *reinforcement* can be profound because these processes can be decisive in close elections, as well as during controversial public debates over issues. Given the Red State–Blue State divide in contemporary U.S. politics, these impacts have broad implications for governance and democracy.

In contrast to the conclusions drawn by Lazarsfeld and his colleagues, subsequent reanalyses of the Erie County and Elmira studies have found evidence of direct news media impact on public cognitions and attitudes.[4] Still, the original studies are noteworthy in that they represent one of the first systematic efforts to examine the impact of news media on public attitudes and because their concept of opinion leadership allowed us to better understand the complementary roles of interpersonal and mass communication in swaying citizens' opinions and attitudes.

New perspectives on media and attitudes

Over time, scholars recognized that some of the assumptions of the limited-effects model had been overstated. The emergence of research in the 1970s showing strong cognitive influence by the news media—research based on such perspectives as agenda-setting, cultivation, and the spiral of silence—eroded the model's influence. It should be noted, however, that even as scholars determined that media could be a critical catalyst in forming and changing public attitudes about a variety of topics in the news, this by no means was a return to a simple direct-effects model. The influence described by these new perspectives was moderated and mediated by a multitude of source, medium, message, audience, and contextual factors. Nonetheless, there also is significant evidence demonstrating strong attitudinal consequences as a result of increased exposure and attention to news content.

Larry Bartels found that methodological and statistical problems contributed to a false assumption of weak attitudinal effects.[5] Specifically, he argued that the influence of prior opinions and attitudes has not been incorporated into most research examining the affective outcomes of news media exposure. In addition, he submits that we can only expect strong media effects when media content deviates substantially from preexisting views or by examining areas where public attitudes are only minimally developed.

Another important factor affecting the scope of media influence on attitudes is the area of political life that is being considered. In particular, research has consistently tracked more consequential links between media exposure and public opinion about foreign affairs than about domestic matters. This trend is partially explained by the fact that citizens have direct personal experience with many areas of domestic policy, but have to rely more heavily on mass media information for their assessments and evaluations of foreign policy issues. In providing a psychological explanation for such patterns, the concept of need for orientation in agenda-setting theory is germane, a concept that suggests that attention to news is highest for subjects that audiences feel are personally relevant, but about which they have great uncertainty.

American college students' opinions of Arab nations and people reflected negative stereotypes portrayed in news media and other mass communication sources.[6] On the other hand, a person's evaluation of the economic well-being of their own country will not only be affected by news coverage, but also by his or her own personal economic situation. In contrast, an individual's position on a war not involving their home country will almost exclusively be based on news media information.

A similar pattern can be found concerning the volatility of

opinions regarding political issues versus political candidates. Benjamin Page and Robert Shapiro's examination of several decades of aggregate public opinion data offered compelling evidence that opinions about public issues tend to be more stable than those regarding public officials.[7] The major public issues are enduring and recurring. Most public officials have shorter appearances in the public-affairs arena.

Among the most comprehensive frameworks for mapping the relationship between news media and political attitudes is John Zaller's RAS model.[8] According to this framework, individuals are affected by the news media to the extent they *Receive* new information (determined by their level of political awareness), the degree to which they *Accept* this information as it is weighed against preexisting opinions and predispositions, and the extent to which it is *Sampled* (this depends on the salient conditions at the point in time they are asked to express their views).

In particular, this model emphasizes the need to account for competing political viewpoints in news content in order to detect strong attitudinal change. As Zaller writes:

> This analysis largely suggests that it is a serious mistake for scholars to conflate *mutually canceling effects* with *non-existent or only "minimal" effects* ... Effects can be very great, even when, as in a tug-of-war, they function to simply cancel out the efforts of the other side.[9]

Consequently, individuals who are modestly attentive to politics may be most influenced by attention to the news in terms of conversion because those at the high end are exposed to a large volume of information, but typically have strong prior opinions that reject contradictory information. On the other hand, those low in attention are not exposed to enough information to shift their assessments. Of course, when information is one-sided, as is often the case in political talk radio, a direct relationship often surfaces between media exposure and opinion preference.[10]

Opinion change is but one type of attitudinal impact that we might expect from the news media on public opinion. The RAS model notes that increases in political awareness are linked with greater attitude stability and strength, an influence that should not be underappreciated. Illustrating this point, Zaller reported that as public awareness of the Vietnam War rose, the number of people who stated they had no opinion on the issue declined. In many areas of public life, exposure and attention to the news media result in increased levels of opinion formation and increased strength of opinions.

An investigation of adolescent political socialization found that attention to the news prompted higher levels of concern about the war in Iraq and more extreme opinions regarding the government's handling of that issue.[11] In another analysis of the impact of television news on the political socialization of adolescents, G. M. Garramone observed that increased television news viewing was connected to higher levels of opinion strength for multiple issues.[12] And David Weaver found that increased media exposure to the federal budget deficit issue was related to strengthened opinions concerning a possible solution to the problem (cutting spending). Notably, the relationship was more robust for attitude strength than for the direction of attitudes.[13]

Differences in the relationships between news coverage and opinion formation also emerge when comparing media channels. During the 2000 U.S. presidential election, Sei-Hill Kim, Dietram Scheufele, and James Shanahan found that higher levels of having an opinion were associated with watching television news and listening to the radio, but not with reading the newspaper.[14]

A related area that also explores the linkages between news media and public attitudes is priming. Building on the concept of agenda setting, priming is a consequence of shifts in the public salience of issues due to the agenda-setting effects of media coverage. According to the priming perspective, the issues and concerns that are highlighted in the news become the standards by which presidents and other politicians are judged. This indirect model of media influence on attitudes and opinions represents a subtle but significant form of impact from news content.

Illustrating this process, the defining issue covered in the news media during the 2008 U.S. presidential election was the economy. Priming theory would predict that voter evaluations of the Democrat and Republican candidates, Barack Obama and John

McCain, would be based on their expected performance concerning this issue. Public opinion polls after the election revealed that the majority of voters selecting Obama rated him as more effective in being able to handle the economy than McCain. Given that polls also showed the economy to be the top public priority for voters, a priming explanation for Obama's 2008 election victory is plausible. Voter preferences might have dramatically differed if their judgments were based on other issues, such as national security or terrorism. Of course, an alternative explanation is that media coverage and political campaign messages were mirroring public concerns, which were driven by the actual state of the economy as the stock market plummeted and unemployment levels rose during the election period.

However, Shanto Iyengar and his associates found robust support for priming effects.[15] In a seminal series of experiments, residents of New Haven, Connecticut, were presented with manipulated television newscasts in order to assess news media impact on audience perceptions. The issues altered were national defense, pollution, and inflation. Among the key findings of these experiments were that news media content not only raised the salience of these political issues—an agenda-setting effect—but that they also affected subsequent evaluations of President Jimmy Carter's job performance. Effects were more pronounced for performance evaluations than for personal assessments of Carter. In another set of experiments in Columbus, Ohio, the priming influence of television news was found on a diverse set of issues, ranging from drug use to unemployment.

In connection with the related concept of second-level agenda setting, scholars also have observed "attribute priming" influence, where shifts in the salience of the attributes of topics in the news affect public evaluations concerning those same topics.[16] Hence, priming processes are not just meaningful for public assessments of political figures, but for other attitude objects in the news as well. Additional details of this influence, particularly for the affective dimension of attributes, are presented in the next chapter's discussion of the affective tone in news reports.

Framing by the mass media also can have important effects on attitude change by altering the weight assigned to information that individuals already have about a topic. This contrasts with belief change, where attitude change occurs by adding information about beliefs associated with a topic. In summarizing the impact of media framing on public attitudes, Thomas Nelson, Zoe Oxley, and Rosalee Clawson assert that

> the mass media, and other institutions of mass political communication, can profoundly influence public opinion *even without any overt attempt at persuasion or manipulation.* The media may sincerely follow institutional norms of impartiality and neutrality, yet they cannot escape the fact that their approach to a story implicitly teaches the public how to understand the central issues. These effects may be wholly unintended, but they are real nonetheless.[17]

Another indirect way the mass media have been found to affect public attitudes is by shaping people's perceptions of what others think. That is, the news media provide a picture of what "others" believe about particular areas of political life. These perceptions of the general public, in turn, alter individual political attitudes and opinions. Evidence supporting this thesis can be found in public opinion research showing that citizen attitudes toward the economy are typically not based on their personal pocketbooks, but by how they believe the economy is performing on a collective level. These perceptions, of course, are determined largely by media portrayals.

Although limited in its application to news, the Elaboration Likelihood Model (ELM), discussed in the previous chapter, can be a useful perspective from which to explain the relationship between news media and public attitudes. While most work on the ELM has examined directly persuasive messages such as advertisements, debates, and speeches, its framework has potential for examining differences in short-term vs. long-term news exposure and differences that might be attributed to different media channels. For example, we might expect greater central processing among newspaper readers due to the heavier emphasis on text, while peripheral cues may be more substantial in television news given its more visual and graphic nature. The newer forms of internet news, such as blogging and social media, also can be explored in this framework.

Normative views on news and public attitudes

A vexing debate about the relationship between news media and citizen opinions and attitudes concerns the extent to which the news media promote democracy and political engagement. Differences among media have been observed for attention to the news and attitudes supporting increased political participation. More specifically, scholarly research on the "video malaise" hypothesis has asserted that exposure to television news decreases support for democratic ideals and participation. According to this view, the content of television news since the 1970s has become more sensationalistic, negative, and oriented toward political strategies for winning rather than toward issues. As a result, the public has heightened attitudes of skepticism and cynicism about politics and government, as well as declining public confidence in the media itself. This trend has been described as "attack journalism," translating into feeding frenzies among reporters who portray politics in a negative and cynical light. Coverage of the Monica Lewinsky sex scandal involving President Bill Clinton may be the quintessential example of this type of reporting. Other trends in news reporting also have implications for making citizens more fearful. For example, exposure to local television news is associated with an increased fear of crime.[18]

Put succinctly by Larry Sabato, "the denial of electoral choice is an obvious consequence of some frenzies, yet the news media's greatest impact on voters is not in the winnowing of candidates, but in the encouragement of cynicism."[19] Offering empirical support for this thesis, Joseph Cappella and Kathleen Hall Jamieson found in a series of experiments that exposure to news oriented toward political strategies and elections as horse races led individuals to have greater distrust and increased cynicism about government and politics.[20] This outcome is not without its price for journalism, as many scholars suggest that the fostering of distrust has contributed to shrinking confidence in the press over the last four decades.

In contrast, some have criticized the primary focus on television news content that typifies this research. Other research has shown that attention to the news activates positive attitudes and opinions regarding political and civic engagement. For example, Robert Putnam, who has been one of the most vocal critics concerning the negative impact of television on civic engagement, argues that newspaper reading is linked to greater interpersonal trust.[21] Using over 20 years of longitudinal data from the General Social Science survey, John Brehm and Wendy Rahn also submit that newspaper reading activates higher levels of trust and confidence in government, while television exposure has the opposite effect.[22]

Kenneth Newton reported that newspaper reading led to more positive attitudes toward politics in England[23] while Christina Holtz-Bacha found parallel trends in Germany. A recent analysis of more than three dozen internet news investigations discovered mixed contributions of news exposure toward civic engagement. [24]

While much of our emphasis here has been on political engagement, it should be noted that news exposure can be a powerful tool for promoting pro-social attitudes and behaviors in other settings, such as health communication efforts for combating AIDS.[25]

Another way that scholars have explored the normative impact of news media in the affective realm of public opinion is by measuring psycho-physiological responses to different types of news content. Again, the major focus has been on broadcast news. One controlled experiment observed that tabloid news production techniques and topic selection are associated with increased levels of perceived and psycho-physiological arousal among audience members.

In addition to differences among the audiences for television and newspapers, the information-processing goals of audience members must also be considered when judging the influence of the news on citizen opinions of political and civic engagement. From a uses-and-gratifications perspective of mass communication, individuals who are active information seekers of political news content show marked increases in levels of trust and confidence in politics with heightened exposure to news.

Conclusion

The relationship between the news media and citizens' attitudes and opinions has been one of ubiquitous concern and complexity among mass communication scholars since the inception of the field. Although historical perspectives have varied on the degree of impact that mass media have, views have broadened. It is now known that opinion formation and reinforcement are as important as opinion change when considering the consequences of news attention. With research trends over the decades sometimes overestimating and then underestimating influence, modern perspectives offer a conditional approach where the impact of news media on citizen attitudes can be profound, but several determinants come into play when considering the precise extent and scope of that influence.

One paramount area meriting future attention involves internet news, social media, and other digital/interactive communication technologies. It also is likely that theoretical perspectives from interpersonal, group, and mass communication will be required in tandem to understand the dynamics of online communication.

8

Tone of the News

Here's the *New York Sewer*! . . . with the best accounts of the markets, and all the shipping news, and four whole columns of country correspondence, and a full account of the Ball at Mrs. White's last night, where all the beauty and fashion of New York was assembled; with the *Sewer*'s own particulars of the private lives of all the ladies that were there! . . . Here's the *Sewer*'s exposure of the Wall Street Gang, and the *Sewer*'s exposure of the Washington Gang, and the *Sewer*'s exclusive account of a flagrant act of dishonesty committed by the Secretary of State when he was eight years old; now communicated, at a great expense, by his own nurse.

Charles Dickens, *The Life & Adventures of Martin Chuzzlewit* (1843)

Although these specific headlines are unfamiliar because they are fictitious, the tone is very familiar. Another media feeding frenzy on the outrage of the day! Journalism has always been about far more than what is sometimes rather prosaically called the surveillance function of the mass media. The *New York Sun* inaugurated the penny press, cheap daily newspapers for a mass audience, because Benjamin Day realized that news filled with great drama and emotion could be harvested from the New York City police courts. Yellow journalism with its daily dose of high emotion arguably reached its peak with the late-nineteenth-century tabloids published by Joseph Pulitzer and William Randolph Hearst. But to this day, daily newspapers, news broadcasts, and other news reports are filled with stories that stir emotion. Even the most serious news coverage frequently has a pervasive emotional tone—most commonly negative. News stories are both denotative messages conveying substantive information and connotative messages conveying tone and emotion.

The New York Times coverage of the issues during the 2000 U.S. presidential election had two distinction dimensions: the visibility of the various issues and the tone of their coverage.[1] Visibility of issues included both the frequency with which they appeared in the news and their prominence on the front page of *The New York Times*. Tone, of course, refers to the positive, negative, or neutral nature of the news about each issue and is sometimes referred to as the affective component of a message. Our previous discussion of the agenda-setting role of the news media examined the transfer of issue salience from the media agenda to the public agenda, a process usually measured in terms of the visibility of issues in the news and in surveys of public opinion. This additional explication of media salience into two dimensions emphasizes the importance of also taking the tone of the news into account.

There are parallel dimensions for the salience of issues among the public.[2] For example, in responding to the frequently used public-opinion question, What is the most important problem facing the country today?, citizens take into account the emotional tone of the issues as well as their substantive aspects—their relevance for society at large and for the individual. All three aspects of the salience of an issue among the public can be measured with sets of semantic differentials, which are seven-point rating scales anchored by various bipolar adjectives. Examples are important—unimportant (social salience); matters to me—doesn't matter to me (personal salience); and exciting—unexciting (emotional salience).

Feelings as compelling arguments

Emotional responses to the news provide an explanation of why exposure to news reports about a topic can result in significant agenda-setting effects. When exposure to news stories about the issue of crime in an experimental setting resulted in increased negative emotions about the issue, people were more likely to consider crime as an important issue facing the nation.[3] More specifically, exposure to news stories that said the crime rate is high and possibly on the rise caused participants in the experiment to be more sad and afraid, emotional responses that in turn increased the likelihood that they regarded crime as an important problem facing the nation. These specific emotional responses mediate—explicate—the relationship between the media agenda and the public agenda, and detail the impact of news coverage on the public's concerns.

Other more global emotional responses in these experiments did not result in a greater likelihood of regarding crime as an important problem facing the nation. Altogether the experiment measured the extent to which participants felt angry, sad, proud, hopeful, happy, and afraid while reading news stories about crime. A general measure of valence was created by summing the responses to the three negative emotions and subtracting the sum of the responses to the three positive responses, and a general measure of arousal was created by summing all six emotional responses regardless of whether they were positive or negative. Neither this general feeling of emotional arousal nor overall valence explains the link between exposure to crime news and naming crime as an important issue facing the nation.

Finding that agenda-setting effects were mediated by two specific emotions, sadness and fear, recalls the concept of *compelling arguments* discussed in Chapter 6. Particular attributes of an issue can have major impact on the salience of that issue for the public. For crime in Texas over a three-year period, the psychological distance between members of the public and the crime reported in the news explained the salience of crime just as well as the total coverage of crime in the news. In the experiments on crime, strong feelings of sadness and fear, which become attributes of the issue of crime for some individuals, arguably became compelling arguments for the importance of the issue of crime.

Images of political candidates

Much of our knowledge about the impact among the public of the news media's attribute agenda, both its substantive and affective aspects, comes from the study of candidate images during elections. The most comprehensive portrait of these attribute agenda-setting effects comes from the 1996 Spanish general election in which the images of three candidates among the public were compared using seven different news media.[4] All 21 correlations were positive with a median value of +.66. This was a particularly demanding test of media effects because the comparisons of the descriptions of the candidates in the media and among citizens were based on 15 categories (5 substantive attributes ×3 affective levels: positive, negative, and neutral). Recall that substantive attributes deal with those aspects of communication messages that help us to cognitively structure various topics while the affective dimension of attributes deals with the positive, neutral, or negative tone present in messages. Taking both the substantive and affective dimensions of the candidate attributes into account results in a comprehensive perspective regarding the influence of news on the images of political candidates among the public.

An election study the previous year in Spain analyzed this agenda-setting impact separately for the substantive and affective dimensions of attributes.[5] For each of these dimensions, there was a monotonic increase in attribute agenda-setting effects with increased exposure to political news in the newspaper or on television. At each level of exposure in either medium, however, the match between the media agenda and the public's descriptions of the candidates was greater for the substantive attributes than for the affective attributes. Nevertheless, even for the affective attributes the median correlation is a robust +.81 in comparison with +.91 for the substantive attributes.

Two elections in Texas, one for governor, the other for U.S. senator, further detailed the role of tone in the news.[6] For all four candidates combined, when both the positive and negative attribute agendas were combined, the match between the media and public images of these candidates was a correlation of +.65.

The median correlation in the 1996 Spanish national election was +.66. When the positive and negative attribute agendas are considered separately for the four Texas candidates, the match between negative attribute agendas was slightly larger, but not by much—a correlation of +.70 versus +.64.

Images and opinions

Both the positive and negative attributes in the public's descriptions of these candidates significantly influenced their opinions about these candidates. For each of the four candidates, both positive and negative attribute agendas held by voters were significant predictors of those voters' opinions about these men. And the voters' negative attribute agendas were stronger predictors of their opinions than their positive attribute agendas, especially in regard to the incumbents seeking reelection as governor and U.S. senator. A separate analysis of the 11 specific attributes of these candidates identified positive mentions of experience and competence as particularly compelling arguments among the public for shaping their opinion of a candidate.

More recently, an analysis of voters' opinions about Hillary Clinton and Barack Obama found that positive attributes in the aggregate describing the emotional traits of the two candidates were significant predictors of voters' opinions, but not negative attributes.[7] Separate analysis of specific attributes identified five positive attributes and three negative attributes as compelling arguments among the public.

The role of certain attributes as compelling arguments also emerged as a consequence of strong attribute agenda-setting effects during the 2006 Israeli national election.[8] This link between the salience of certain attributes for voters and their opinions about major party leaders' suitability for office was stronger for heavy newspaper readers than for light newspaper readers. For example, among light readers only two attributes, leadership and lack of morality, significantly predicted evaluations of Ehud Olmert, while among heavy readers, five attributes—leadership, lack of morality, intelligence, lack of credibility, and credibility—significantly predicted his evaluations. Across all three party leaders, only two attributes—one positive and one negative—were compelling arguments for their suitability for office among light newspaper readers. Among heavy newspaper readers, there were ten instances of compelling arguments—six positive and four negative. Substantively, credibility, intelligence, leadership, and morality were the dominant attributes that predicted voters' evaluations.

Tone of candidate coverage

During the 2000 U.S. presidential election, trends in the standings of George Bush and Al Gore in the Gallup polls from March until Election Day were significantly linked to the pattern of news coverage.[9] Both the cumulative salience of the candidates—the proportion of news coverage that each man received over time—and the cumulative affective attribute salience of the candidates—the average tone of the news coverage over time—explained the level of candidate support among the public found in these 20 Gallup polls across the election year.

In the final three months of the 1992 and 1996 U.S. presidential elections, the tone of television news coverage influenced day-to-day swings in the candidates' standings in the polls.[10] Favorable coverage of Republican campaign events on national television increased support for the Republican candidate. Conversely, favorable coverage of the Democrat campaign decreased support for the Republican candidate. The strength of these affective media effects on voters' opinions was similar in both election years.

Another longitudinal investigation of national news media coverage and public opinion about the president suggests that the tone of news content is a key predictor of presidential job approval.[11] Moreover, this impact is pronounced during times when international and foreign policy matters are at the forefront of media content.[12]

In Germany, the tone of the news about Helmut Kohl influenced public opinion about his performance between 1975 and 1984, first as leader of the opposition and subsequently as chancellor.[13] The median correlation between the tone of the coverage in six major newspapers and news magazines and the public's opinions across those years was +.48.

Spanish citizens' ratings of six major political figures on a 10-point scale ranging from "highly unfavorable" to "highly favorable" were compared with their descriptions of these men in response to the widely used question, "Suppose that you had a friend who had been away for a long time and knew nothing about [name of political figure]. What would you tell them?" [14] Responses to this question were coded on a five-point affective scale ranging from very negative to very positive. For these six political figures, the correlations between the public's affective attribute agenda and their opinions for each of these men ranged from +.78 to +.97. To borrow a phrase from Walter Lippmann's *Public Opinion*, knowledge about the pictures in our heads, especially the affective component of those pictures, also is very revealing of our opinions.

Finally, in considering the influence of the news media on the shaping of public opinion about public figures, the most common scenario is that the basic agenda-setting effect—media salience (prominence in the news) influences public salience (recognition of those figures)—in turn translates into holding opinions about these public figures. Another possibility, however, is that media salience leads to holding opinions, which subsequently prompt increased public salience. This alternative sequence of effects is especially likely when audience involvement is low. In addition, related research on "mere exposure" indicates that simple message repetition can produce shifts in opinion (with minimal impact on cognitions) concerning low-involvement attitude objects. Strong evidence for this alternative model was found in the American public's awareness of and opinions about 11 major political figures during the 1996 presidential election.[15]

Tone of issue coverage

Returning to the traditional domain of agenda-setting effects, the influence of news coverage on the salience of issues among the public: there is significant evidence about the important role of affect in the formation of public opinion in a longitudinal investigation of the effects of economic-news coverage across five Israeli elections for the Knesset between 1988 and 2003.[16] As expected, the sheer volume of media coverage on the economy created a significant agenda-setting effect, increasing the likelihood of people naming "the economy" as the most important problem facing the country. Adding the tone of this coverage almost doubles the impact of news coverage. Recall that these are the two dimensions of media salience discussed at the beginning of this chapter, and both dimensions of the news about the economy also significantly influenced voters' opinions about the economic performance of the incumbent political party.

Not surprisingly, the state of the economy, with its direct implications for nearly every member of the public, is one of the issues frequently found center stage in public opinion. Although personal experience obviously has a major impact on the salience of this issue, news coverage of broader aspects of the economy ranging from unemployment levels to government budget deficits also can have extensive impact on public opinion. Negative news about the economy is generally far more newsworthy and prevalent than good news, and negative headlines influence the public's perceptions and opinions about the future health of the economy. In turn, consumers adjust their buying behavior to fit these perceptions: gloomy news about the economy becomes a self-fulfilling prophecy.

Issues and public figures are not the only attitude objects affected by the tone of news coverage. This is true for many of the other pictures in our heads as well. The frequency of news reports about foreign countries is highly correlated with the public's perception of whether the United States has a vital interest in those countries. When asked to rate 21 different countries on a 100-point "feeling thermometer," however, people's ratings of these countries showed no correspondence with either the positive or neutral tone of the television news coverage for these countries, but demonstrated a highly significant link between their ratings and negative news coverage of these countries.[17]

Negative political advertising

The tone of the news and other mass media messages is frequently emphasized in discussions of political campaigns, particularly the widespread use of negative political ads at all levels of politics. Although much of this discussion is normative, decrying the presence of so many attack ads on television and their negative implications for healthy political dialogue and deliberation as mainstays of democracy, there also have been significant scholarly attempts to measure the impact of negative political ads on many facets of public opinion.

By way of preface, there is considerable evidence suggesting that messages with a negative tone, whether news or political ads or whatever, are better remembered by people and have a greater impact on impression formation. Also, it must be noted that the heavy use of negative political advertising is a fairly recent phenomenon in the half-century history of campaigning via television ads. From 1952 through 2004, a total of 14 U.S. presidential elections, on average 59 percent of the ads were positive and 41 percent were negative.[18] It was 1984 before any candidate's campaign ads were more negative than positive. In that election, 54 percent of Walter Mondale's ads were negative. Eight years later, two-thirds of both George Bush's and Bill Clinton's ads were negative. With a few exceptions, this heavy use of negative advertising has continued.

The impact of these ads on voters varies considerably when the characteristics of both the candidates and voters are taken into account. For example, negative attacks on a candidate's issue positions can be effective among some voters, but not all. The major area of debate about the impact of negative ads has centered on political participation, particularly voter turnout on Election Day.

Under some circumstances it appears that negative ads can alienate citizens and depress voter turnout. However, recent investigations have concluded that this impact is limited at best and that all in all negative advertising may actually arouse greater interest in a campaign and stimulate increased voter participation and turnout.

Political ads on television often make creative use of visuals to convey tone and emotion, but the visual components of the news on TV also can convey tone and emotion.[19] Detailed analysis of the positive and negative facial expressions, posture, and gestures of George Bush and Al Gore in TV news reports during the 2000 U.S. presidential campaign found significantly more shots displaying these positive nonverbal behaviors by Gore than Bush and significantly more shots displaying these negative behaviors by Bush than Gore. And the National Election Study found significant differences between Bush and Gore in the public's opinion of the candidates' positive and negative affective attributes. Most important, these differences in public opinion were significantly correlated with exposure to positive media portrayals of both Bush and Gore's nonverbal behavior and to negative media portrayals of Bush's nonverbal behavior.

Conclusion

The agenda-setting theory of the news media spotlights their influence on which issues gain public attention and come to be regarded as particularly important. Introduction of an additional level of media effects, attribute agenda-setting, expanded our focus from the influence of the news media on what to think about to include how to think about it. In other words, news coverage not only directs our attention to certain objects—public issues, political figures, and so on; the news also directs our attention to particular attributes of those objects—aspects of issues, characteristics of political figures, and more.

Agenda-setting theory clearly identifies two dimensions of these attributes: a cognitive component regarding information about specific substantive traits or characteristics that describe the object and an affective component regarding the positive, negative, or neutral tone of these descriptions on the news agenda or the public agenda. Until recently, however, far more attention was paid to the substantive attributes defining public issues or the images of public figures than to the tone of those traits. Japanese scholar Toshio Takeshita concluded that this lack of attention to feelings and tone was an unintended consequence of describing agenda-setting effects as cognitive effects in order to contrast them with the earlier efforts during the 1940s and 1950s to find media effects on attitudes and opinions. In a more sweeping indictment of a widespread and longstanding cultural bias, Drew Westen in *The Political Brain* declares that "the vision of mind that has captured the imagination of philosophers, cognitive scientists, economists, and political scientists since the eighteenth century—a *dispassionate mind* that makes decisions by weighing the evidence and reasoning to the most valid conclusions—bears no relation to how the mind and brain actually work."[20]

At a minimum, the rational-person model of human behavior needs to be complemented with an emotional-person model of human behavior. This chapter has identified aspects of this emotional-person model in dimensions of the media and public agendas and discussed the role of emotions, particularly negative emotions, in influencing the public's response to a variety of issues and the public's images of political candidates and political parties. In turn, these concerns about issues and images of candidates have direct implications for the public's attitudes and opinions regarding these issues and political candidates.

9

Political Behavior

While voting is often criticized as a very narrow indicator of political activity, many perspectives of democracy and civic engagement argue that it represents the most basic and fundamental form of citizen action. And it is further argued that the news media should serve as a catalyst for motivating this action. The performance of news media in generating voter turnout is quite mixed, however. Sometimes exposure to the news is a positive force for voting; at other times its role is the opposite, such as when projected outcomes are reported on election night.[1]

As we discussed earlier regarding news media influence on public attitudes, the early research on the impact of mass communication on political behavior initially assumed massive effects only to later shift to predicting minimal or no effects. Examining the impact of mass media on voter conversion during the 1940 and 1948 U.S. presidential elections, Lazarsfeld and his associates concluded that exposure to the news media reinforced existing preferences for candidates rather than stimulating large swings from one candidate to another.[2] In addition, they underscored the importance of interpersonal communication in shaping vote choice. Of course, it is critical to note that reinforcement effects are meaningful, and in some cases can determine election outcomes.

While the relationship between the use of mass media and interpersonal discussion as two forms of civic participation has not been extensively examined in the past, it has received increased attention in recent years. The role of the media in stimulating political conversation and deliberation has gotten particular notice. Attention to the news is correlated with greater discussion about politics, but the causal direction of this linkage remains unclear. One school of thought posits that media exposure provides cognitive resources to citizens that enable them to feel comfortable discussing politics with family and peers, an activity that engenders closer ties to the community and ultimately translates into civic participation.[3] Information efficacy may be especially relevant here because it suggests that individuals will not actively participate in politics until they believe they have a sufficient level of information to feel competent.

Of course, there is also the possibility that discussion may lead to greater news exposure, and there is some evidence supporting this view in studies of adolescents, and for topics that are highly involving. From this perspective, discussion of politics may generate greater interest in public affairs, leading citizens to actively seek out information via mass media channels. The social utility of news media use for anticipated political conversation prompts citizens who discuss politics frequently to pay more attention to news.[4] Given the conflicting research findings, we conclude that the relationship between news attention and discussion is probably best characterized as *reciprocal* and *shared,* where increases in one type of political communication is tied to increases in the other. What is important here is that these increases in all forms of political communication are core antecedents of political participation.

Over time, the news media have come to be recognized as a paramount force in shaping participation, but the relationship is complicated and is by no means universal across news channels and audiences. In addition to media influence, demographic characteristics (age and level of education, for instance), sociological determinants (neighborhood diversity, living in urban versus rural areas, and similar factors), and political predispositions (for example, interest in politics and party identification) also have been identified as key factors affecting many types of civic action.

Regarding channel factors, exposure to newspapers and print media in general is connected with a greater propensity to vote in elections than exposure to other communication channels. Comparing the influence of different channels on voter turnout during the 1980 U.S. presidential election, Lyman Kellstedt found that paying attention to newspapers increased voter turnout levels, although exposure to radio and magazines was also beneficial, albeit to a smaller degree.[5] In the 1992 U.S. presidential election, attention to newspapers increased intentions to vote, but the same result was not detected for television news.[6] This result was present even after controlling for traditional demographic and political predictors. And the 1996 U.S. presidential election again confirmed the mobilizing influence of newspaper reading on voting.[7] Given its consistent influence in facilitating turnout over many decades, the current trend of declining newspaper readership and the sustainability of the newspaper industry itself are of considerable concern in regard to participatory democracy.

A comparison of the influence of various mass media on local participation found that newspaper reading was more influential than paying attention to television.[8] One reason for this pattern is that newspapers contain more "mobilizing information" that citizens can directly use for political action and behavior. This, of course, underscores that the content of news—in addition to channel characteristics—is another factor affecting the extent of news media influence on behavior.

Two major ways in which content can activate participation are by arousing interest in politics and by increasing knowledge among citizens so they feel empowered to act. For example, an analysis of the 2004 U.S. presidential election showed that exposure to television, radio, and television news predicted political interest while internet news exposure increased political knowledge.[9] Taking the next step to participation, increased political interest induced a greater likelihood of voting, and there was a positive relationship between political knowledge and voting.

Further elaborating the role of content, Sei-Hill Kim and Miejeong Han noted the important distinction between news and entertainment media. Surveying citizens in Seoul, Korea, they noted that attention to newspapers and television news encouraged voting and political discussion among respondents, but watching television for entertainment depressed turnout.[10]

Heightened cynicism and greater emphasis on the horse-race aspect of campaigns in news, however, are believed to decrease efficacy and increase cynicism among citizens by overwhelming them with negative information, thereby indirectly reducing participation levels. As Thomas Patterson argues, "By emphasizing the game dimension day after day, the press forces it to the forefront, strengthening the voters' mistrust of the candidates and reducing their sense of involvement."[11]

Many of these content trends are particularly pronounced in television news. Putnam's perspective on social capital, for instance, suggests that television is the primary culprit in decreasing civic and political participation. More television watching means less of virtually every form of civic participation and social involvement. Other things being equal, Putnam noted, each additional hour of television viewing means roughly a 10 percent reduction in most forms of civic activism—fewer public meetings, fewer local committee members, fewer letters to Congress, and so on.[12]

Although there is some evidence for Putnam's assertions about general television viewing, empirical support for the negative consequences of television news exposure on behavior has been inconclusive. Sometimes attention to television news is a precursor to civic participation, though not to the same extent as attention to newspapers.

In addition to media channels and content factors, audience characteristics can modify the extent of news media impact on participation. People who are active seekers of political information exhibit higher levels of participation than those who are passive information processors. Active information seeking via print, broadcast, or internet news leads to increased engagement, as heavy media users may benefit at a proportionately greater rate than light media users.

With the rise of interactive and digital media, some view digital communications as optimistic tools that will ultimately allow for direct democracy in the image of the Athenian marketplace.

Taking this optimistic view, Erik Bucy and Kimberly Gregson argue:

> A principal component of the new media is the notion of political interactivity, or mediated real-time feedback between political actors and citizens. A primary feature setting interactive media apart from traditional campaign news coverage or political advertising is the potential for spontaneous interaction among political figures, journalists and citizens.[13]

Others take a more skeptical outlook, asserting that the new media represent additional tools through which the establishment maintains the status quo.

Exploring the impact of new media empirically, one investigation of internet news found that exposure engendered higher levels of voter turnout during the 1996, 1998, and 2000 U.S. national elections, even after controlling for a number of established behavioral determinants, such as demographics and political interest.[14] On the other hand, Gang Han found that simple exposure to internet news was not associated with higher levels of voter turnout during the 2000 U.S. presidential election. He did find, however, that when users went online to actively seek out information about politics, this increased their likelihood of voting. The information-processing strategy that individuals use when going online for news again seems to wield considerable influence on voter turnout.[15]

Shifting from the act of voting, the possibility that attention and exposure to news can lead to significant effects on vote *choice* as well also have been examined. These questions are of central concern to the profession of journalism, given its values of autonomy, neutrality, and objectivity. In an examination of 9,256 towns across the United States from 1996 to 2000, Stefano DellaVigna and Ethan Kaplan investigated how the introduction of Fox News into cable markets shifted voting behavior toward Republican candidates. Their results indicated that the Republican vote grew significantly in these communities for both presidential and Senate elections.[16]

To provide some context to these findings, it is crucial to recognize that systematic analyses of news content across a variety of channels and contexts have failed to uncover any consistent partisan bias favoring certain political parties or groups. Other content patterns have been observed, such as the tendency to overly rely on government sources, to provide greater access to political incumbents, and to limit the voice of political groups not embedded within the traditional two-party system in the United States. Many critics have blamed news media for the lack of a viable third party in the American political system.

While a nonpartisan media system typically is assumed in the United States, this is not necessarily the case in other countries. One study in Britain traced the influence of newspapers in shifting voter behavior during the 1992 and 1997 national elections.[17] Unlike traditional models in which general newspaper reading confers greater voter turnout, this investigation discovered that voters who read newspapers consistent with their partisan preferences voted with greater frequency than those who read newspapers inconsistent with their partisan preferences. As such, partisan news circulation can potentially determine election outcomes and results, particularly in highly competitive races. Subtle reinforcement effects can produce lasting changes in the political system despite small amounts of actual voter conversion. Illustrating this, Thomas Holbrook found that media coverage of conventions, debates, and other campaign events influenced voter selection during the 1984, 1988, and 1992 U.S. presidential elections even after controlling for political predispositions and economic forces.[18]

Beyond traditional hard news content, scholars also have explored the role of explicitly persuasive messages in the news media, such as editorial endorsements and political commentary. One longitudinal study from 1940–2002 found that newspaper endorsements have moved away from Republican candidates (which was the historical trend) to more balanced selections in recent years, though incumbents receive endorsements at a greater rate than challengers.[19] And these endorsements affect voters' behavior on Election Day. Combining a content analysis of editorial positions and exit poll data during the 2000 Senate election race in Minnesota, James Druckman and Michael Parkin found that voter decisions were largely based on endorsements of candidates by the newspapers through which they received their primary political information.[20]

The proliferation of media channels has widened participation gaps, as individuals highly interested in public affairs consume more political information than ever before while individuals not interested in public affairs more easily avoid political information given the plethora of entertainment options that are now available.[21] When there were fewer channels from which to select, even those individuals who were not interested in politics were still inadvertently exposed to some news and consequently experienced some of its impact on participation.

Offering an indirect explanation of the relationship between the news media and voter behavior, priming theory not only explains news media influence on attitudes, but also on vote choice. As a consequence of agenda-setting, news media help define the criteria by which political leaders and policies are evaluated in public opinion through their emphasis on certain issues and topics in presenting the news. Using the presidency as an example, when the news highlights the economy, public judgments about the president tend to be based on his perceived performance on that issue. By extension, media emphasis on certain issues and topics also can shape voting behavior.

In the 2000 Senate election in Minnesota, Druckman demonstrated that vote choice was affected by the salience of issues and candidate images in the news consumed by attentive voters.[22] Similar results have been found in Israeli and Canadian elections.[23] And among adolescents, media use and discussion not only increased the salience of issues, but also crystallized political attitudes and orientations that shaped first-time voting.[24]

Marilyn Roberts was able to correctly classify which candidate citizens voted for during the 1990 Texas gubernatorial election based on their perceived level of concern about various political issues.[25] Her results indicated that a two-step behavioral process of agenda setting operates, whereby the salience of issues in the news raises their importance to voters, who then use their level of concern with those issues to make vote choices.

Impacts on other forms of participation

Just as voting or attending a public meeting represents traditional civic participation, political participation also includes behaviors such as volunteering or donating to a cause and more controversial forms of action such as attending a political protest or boycotting an organization. Michael Delli Carpini asserts that "ultimately, the democratically engaged are citizens who *act*—through voting and other forms of electoral involvement, contacting public officials, membership in civic organizations, volunteering in their community, or even protesting and demonstrating."[26] News media can serve as a major impetus in stimulating many different forms of political participation.

A comparison of volunteer activities among different racial groups in two Missouri communities found an indirect relationship between attention to the news and public action.[27] Exposure to local news media triggered increased membership in many different types of associations (political, civic, religious, and so forth), which motivated greater willingness among citizens to volunteer in their local communities. This pattern was similar for both African-Americans and whites. A subsequent analysis of residents in Columbia, Missouri, also found that attention to local news media and internet use predicted associational membership, and that this relationship was mediated by the information processing strategies of audiences.[28] This linkage between attention to the news and volunteering is not limited to secular participation. Subscribing to a newspaper also is correlated with membership and active involvement in churches.[29] Because many individuals are active in civic and political matters through churches and other religious organizations, the impact of such behavioral influence should not be underestimated.

Using an agenda-setting framework, David Weaver explored the impact of mass media in shaping not just the public salience of issues, but a larger range of behaviors as well.[30] Among Indiana residents, increased salience of the federal budget deficit issue was connected with voting, as well as actions such as signing a petition and attending a public meeting. Altering the cognitive priorities of citizens via mass media exposure can encourage many types of participation.

Similar to the effects on voting, channel and content differences influence the impact of news media on other types of participation. Putnam's assertions concerning the negative consequences of television on social capital has unfavorable implications for political participation, but the preponderance of empirical support for such outcomes concerns general television viewing rather than attention to news. Watching television news enhances many types of political participation.

In her analysis of a national sample of 15,000 U.S. citizens, Pippa Norris found that watching public affairs on television news prompted higher levels of campaign contributions, organizational membership, and informal community involvement.[31] And reading the newspaper was tied to higher levels of working for political campaigns, making financial contributions, contacting politicians, and joining organizations. General television viewing was negatively related to informal community involvement, while listening to the radio was not connected to any type of political participation.

In another study of the 2004 U.S. presidential election, television news exposure had positive effects on both civic and political participation.[32] Political participation includes behaviors such as attending a political meeting or working on a campaign, while civic participation involves behaviors such as attending a protest or contacting a public official. These findings regarding television news exposure were consistent with reading the newspaper and listening to radio news as well. Online political information use only predicted civic participation overall, but it did affect political participation among those who were highly interested in politics.

Looking at radio, the oldest form of broadcast media, the influence of political talk radio, in particular, has been considered a prominent force in eliciting public behavior through such actions as letter writing campaigns, protesting, and consumer boycotts. The interactive and dialogic nature of such media formats fuels their ability to spur political action compared to other formats and channels. One study of the 1992 U.S. presidential election found that listening to or participating in call-in radio and television news programs was associated with great political efficacy.[33] Internet use—also notable for its dialogic and interactive nature—is strongly linked to political donations, as demonstrated by the successful fundraising efforts of Howard Dean and Barack Obama during the 2004 and 2008 U.S. presidential campaigns respectively.

On the other hand, critics have contended that exposure to talk radio and internet news ultimately disengages listeners by polarizing their opinions and raising their cynicism toward politics. Diana Mutz suggests that individuals exposed to information and communication networks consistent with their political beliefs are more likely to engage in political action, while those exposed to heterogeneous perspectives are more likely to deliberate about their political participation, an action that can ultimately decrease their overall engagement.[34] In terms of quality, however, participation based on heterogeneous viewpoints is likely to be more informed and rational. These are issues with substantial implications for conceptions of democratic participation that merit further explication.

Turning to long-term political socialization, television news can act as a powerful stimulus for participation among children, young adults, and immigrants. Some advantages of television news that may explain this influence are its accessibility, reach, and the ease with which information can be processed and integrated cognitively. Television news especially can function as a portal into the political system for new immigrant populations who are just developing the language and literacy skills required to receive information through newspapers, magazines, and the internet.

For adolescents and younger audiences, electronic media may serve as more important catalysts for civic participation than print media. Examining media use and civic activity among a national sample of 14- to 22-year-olds, Josh Pasek, Kate Kenski, Daniel

Romer, and Kathleen Jamieson found significant relationships among national television news viewing, listening to radio news, using the internet for political information, and civic behaviors.[35] While reading newspapers did not stimulate increased civic activity, reading magazines was a positive factor.

In more controversial settings, scholars have examined the extent to which news media promote unconventional forms of political expression such as protesting and boycotting. The role of alternative media is vital to understanding this type of political behavior. Among residents of Wichita, Kansas, exposure to alternative media was not only associated with gains in conventional participation such as voting, but with unconventional participation such as attending a political protest.[36] Attention to television news and newspapers was not connected to the more unconventional types of behavior, implying that different media channels may translate into different kinds of participation. One explanation for this pattern is that traditional news media tend to portray protest and similar types of participation in unfavorable terms,[37] whereas people who engaged in both conventional and unconventional forms of participating also were heavy users of both traditional and alternative media.

The influence of mass media on all forms of participation is enhanced during times of national crisis because of the increased attention to news and the generally uniform content that is presented—in terms of both volume and tone. Individuals who participated in online communities after the 9/11 terrorist attacks were more likely to attend public meetings, volunteer for relief activities, and write letters to news media than those who did not.[38] This impact during crises is not the same for all types of news audiences or kinds of participation, however. Among Iraq War dissenters, antiwar actions were predicted by heightened levels of internet news use, which were driven by feelings of disapproval with mainstream media presentations of the war.[39] The internet functioned as an alternative news source for those not satisfied with traditional media portrayals of public affairs.

In an international context, mass media have contributed to the development of social movements and change in many settings.

Gadi Wolfsfeld's extensive analysis of Israeli politics found that mass media were often a primary force in inducing political activity in the form of protesting and demonstrating.[40] The media's role was most powerful, however, for groups with limited resources.

The emergence of digital media and interactive communications has accelerated the pace at which such social change occurs. A study of the pro-East Timor mobilization movement in Portugal describes the significant role of mass media and digital communications in generating a variety of public responses in both online and offline political activism.[41] In the U.S., internet use predicted people's willingness to attend international events and to volunteer with international causes and issues.[42] One reason for the marked impact of the media on public actions concerned with international issues is that they serve as the chief source of information on foreign affairs. In domestic affairs, personal experience and interpersonal communication play a larger part. Notably, the synergy between traditional news media and the use of the internet as a tool for facilitating social change offers new opportunities for unconventional forms of participation and grassroots efforts that have not been available in the past.

Conclusion

While studies in the early days of communication research initially suggested a limited impact of mass media on political behavior, more contemporary research has shown that news media can directly and indirectly shape political action. This influence is not universal, however, and it is constrained by several factors. When thinking about the behavioral consequences of mass communication, it is important to take a broad-ranging perspective that not only includes formal actions such as voting, but informal activities such as volunteering, protesting, and making donations.

Given the blurring lines among mass, organizational, and interpersonal communication in online settings, it is important to consider a broad variety of theoretical perspectives. And with globalization now a prominent force in the ever-changing media landscape, and its implications for political behavior, broad comparative investigations across political and media systems are needed as well.[43] Both types of comparisons are important contextual forces to consider when studying the behavioral consequences of news.

10

What Citizens Bring to the News

People react differently to the news media. For some, these media provide content that has a great impact on their knowledge, attitudes, and behavior. For others, the news plays a minor role in their daily lives. The fact that people use and react differently to the news media means that there is a vast profusion of possibilities to examine. What are the keys to differential learning patterns among people? What are the differences among individuals that act as contingent conditions for agenda-setting? What types of news consumers are attracted to certain news media content, while other individuals avoid exposure to the news altogether?

The most common approach to identifying individual differences among groups of people examines demographic characteristics: differences based on people's age, gender, level of education, income, and so on. Fred Kerlinger notes that demographics have been used "to assess social conditions and social change, to monitor the achievement of governmental social goals and to study human and social conditions in order to understand and improve them."[1] A number of these basic characteristics of people consistently have been found to affect individuals' exposure to the news media. They form a necessary stage on which media effects can appear. We know that traditionally people who read newspapers tend to have higher education and income levels and are older. Other individual differences influencing media use are political involvement, feelings of civic duty, and frequency of interpersonal communication.

Whether media use and some demographic variables are related, however, is not clear-cut. Research examining racial differences, for instance, has produced mixed results. On the one hand, Virginia Fielder and Leonard Tipton found that minority groups use newspapers less than whites.[2] However, Gilbert Cranberg and Vincent Rodriguez found that the percentage of minority readers of newspapers mirrors the U.S. population.[3]

Other research has found little difference between men and women in the amount of media used, though topics of interest do vary by gender. Women tend to be higher readers of newspaper advice columns, fashion and food sections, display ads and coupons. Men tend to be higher readers of sports and business news. However, Gerald Stone notes that the overlap in readership for some of these categories is extensive.[4] The differences between male and female readers may be shrinking as sports departments have increased their coverage of women's sports, and fashion and food sections have moved to more gender-neutral coverage.

Most of the demographic and attitudinal factors leading to news exposure suggest that people are active processors of news media content and demonstrate that people have a great deal of control over their exposure to the media and the subsequent effects from that exposure. Finally, one demographic variable that has been under-examined is religion. Clearly, religion plays a role in opinion formation on issues such as abortion. John Evans found religion was a factor in respondents' stands on the issue of human cloning. Evangelicals were more opposed to cloning and more likely to see cloning as a religious issue.[5]

Early audience debates

In the early decades of public opinion research, individuals were thought to be passive processors of information. Individuals had little control over what they were exposed to and thus had little control over the effects of exposure to mass media. This notion of a passive audience seemed logical at that time since media choices were limited and the content in the media was relatively homogeneous. In addition, the popularity of radio and television supported the belief that media had powerful effects over all individuals. From this perspective, media messages injected themselves into media consumers, and their influences spread throughout society. Media effects were seen as a kind of hypodermic needle.

The idea of a passive audience continued into later years, when both radio and television were often used as "background noise." Individuals would turn on the radio or television, but pay minimal attention to what was being aired. Nevertheless, there also was evidence of powerful media influence from the earliest days. The Payne Fund studies in the 1930s examined media influences on children, and their findings caused serious concerns among parents. And Orson Welles's radio broadcast of his dramatization of H. G. Wells' novel *The War of the Worlds* in 1938 led to panic among many members of its American audience. Most of the research today has abandoned the passive-audience model in favor of an active-audience approach. This approach was greatly enhanced with the introduction of an expanded uses and gratifications perspective in the 1970s.

Uses and gratifications

The uses and gratifications perspective can be traced back to the 1940s, when some researchers looked at what individuals did with media content, rather than what media content did to people. This approach is based on the idea that individuals have certain needs that they use the media to gratify. The specific needs vary among individuals, of course, as well as the degree to which the needs are gratified.

Elihu Katz, Jay Blumler, and Michael Gurevitch proposed a model of uses and gratifications that involved "(a) the social and psychological origins of (b) needs, which generate (c) expectations of (d) the mass media or other sources, which lead to (e) differential patterns of media exposure (or engagement in other activities), resulting in (f) need gratifications, and (g) other consequences, perhaps mostly unintended ones."[6]

Phillip Palmgreen described uses and gratifications as being concerned with "(a) gratifications and media consumption; (b) social and psychological origins of gratifications; (c) gratifications and media effects; (d) gratifications sought and obtained (e) expectancy-value approaches to uses and gratifications; and (f) audience activity."[7]

The key to uses and gratifications thinking is that individuals are active in selecting what content, and in which medium, they will be exposed to. This purposive exposure is meant to fill a need. Further, it is argued that mass media content cannot have an effect on a person who has no use for these media or their content. A variety of motivations have been examined in uses and gratifications theory. Motivations such as surveillance, diversion, interaction, and action have all been linked with purposive media use. *Surveillance* has been measured through survey questions dealing with whether respondents believe the news media allow them to keep up with political happenings, judge what political leaders are really like, judge who is likely to win an election, and understand what is going on in politics. Explorations of *diversion* ask respondents if they use the media to pass time or to enjoy the excitement of an election race. *Interaction* questions ask if the news media help them develop ammunition for political arguments or prepare them for future political discussions. A focus on *action* asks respondents if media help them decide if they will vote or to make up their mind how to vote.

Several key trends have been found regarding uses and gratifications. Age, for instance, plays an important role. Senior citizens use the media for companionship and to overcome boredom. College students use media for guidance and to see the ideas and lifestyles of others. Children tend to use media mainly for entertainment. Moreover, gender differences have also been found. Women tend to use television for self-identity, social contact, and entertainment, while men use television for information, entertainment, and diversion.

Researchers also have applied the uses and gratifications approach to internet use. During presidential campaigns, Barbara Kaye and Thomas Johnson found that political use of the internet is slightly different based on the purpose behind the use.[8] The internet provides a wide variety of content, including web pages, newspapers, and journals, bulletin boards, electronic mailing lists, and chat rooms. Certainly, with such a wide variety of content, motivations for use of these internet tools can vary greatly across individuals [9]

Through the years, the uses and gratifications perspective also has been criticized for its limitations. First, critics note that research in this area is dependent upon self-reports. This assumes that individuals can identify and estimate their own motivations for using the mass media. Individuals must be aware of the reasons they use the media and must be able to articulate these reasons. Second, gratifications sought are not necessarily predictive of gratifications obtained. Much research has concentrated on the gratifications sought without determining if the reason behind the media use was fulfilled. If a motivation is not successfully fulfilled, future media use patterns could change. Two other criticisms are worth noting. Critics note a lack of clarity in the key terms of this perspective that hampers analysis and discussion. "Gratifications," "motives," and "needs" are often used interchangeably. In addition, critics question whether individuals are aware enough of their media usage patterns to be able to describe their motivations for this use. Despite these criticisms, uses and gratifications has been a useful approach. Perhaps the most effective use of this approach is when it is merged with the analysis of media effects. Motivations for using mass media should play a role in the effects of that media use.

This merger of perspectives proved especially appropriate in agenda-setting. David Weaver, notably, first proposed a linkage between uses and gratifications and effects with his concept of need for orientation.[10] The goal in this early agenda-setting research was to identify the psychological reasons that enhance or inhibit agenda-setting effects. As discussed in Chapter 5, the greater the need for orientation, the greater the use of news media and the stronger are the agenda-setting effect. More recently, Jörg Matthes examined the role played by the need for orientation in both first- and second-level agenda-setting and found that need for orientation explains the amount of information sought by individuals, but not the tone of the information that people are searching for.[11] Thus, need for orientation works in the first level of agenda-setting, but is less important in the second level.

Media dependency

Related to uses and gratifications is the concept of *media dependency*, which also posits an active audience using the mass media for specific purposes. Media dependency, however, goes one step further and suggests that the motivations to use mass media have become more varied and more acute. In first proposing the theory, Sandra Ball-Rokeach and Melvin DeFleur argued that fewer traditional interpersonal sources are available to individuals as a society increases in complexity.[12] Thus, individuals turn to the media for useful information. Motivations lead to media use, as with uses and gratifications research. However, media dependency researchers argue that media usage is increasing and replacing personal contact. This theoretical approach, then, integrates audiences, media and the social system, and has more of a macro-social perspective than is found in traditional uses and gratifications research.

This trend toward greater dependency on the media is based on several factors. Individuals are goal-oriented, and they have basic needs for information about things such as finding food or making political decisions. In traditional societies much of these information needs were gratified by word of mouth. In complex societies, with social differences in ethnicity, occupation specialization, and economic class, word of mouth channels are weak. Thus, people in these complex social systems become highly dependent upon mass media for information.

Factors affecting the magnitude of dependency on media include an individual's need for information and the availability of information elsewhere. Generally speaking, the greater the dependency on media, the more likely the media content will alter the cognitions, attitudes and behaviors of individuals. Furthermore, people become more dependent on media that meet many needs more than on media that meet just a few. Media dependency also increases during times of change and high conflict, when individuals rely on the media for information to clear up confusion.

Patterns of selective behavior

An additional complication in understanding the formation of public opinion involves each individual's subjective mental processing of the news. Four major concepts describe how people process media messages.

Selective exposure

Individuals decide which media they will be exposed to. This, of course, is the basis of the uses and gratifications perspective. People can make conscious decisions about media use based on certain needs. They will selectively expose themselves to certain media while avoiding others. Factors affecting media exposure include previous media use, attitudes toward a medium, the mood of the individual, and personal feelings regarding avoidance or involvement with a particular topic.

Selective attention

Individuals decide which media messages they will attend to. Individuals may be exposed to a certain message, but they do not necessarily pay attention to that message. Selective attention involves which information is processed and which is ignored. People tend to avoid messages that produce dissonance—information that is counter to their values and beliefs—and to attend to information that matches previously processed information.

The term "selective attention" often is used interchangeably with two related concepts, "working/primary memory" and "awareness." Attention implies some degree of in-depth processing of a message, and attention to the news media is a stronger predictor of media effects than exposure.

Selective retention

Given the wealth of information available, individuals have limited memory capacity and therefore cannot retain all of the information that they are exposed to. Through selective retention unwanted information is eliminated. Often, this means that individuals retain messages that reinforce their previously held attitudes and purge information that is in contrast to their interests, values, and beliefs. This results in the reduction of cognitive dissonance.

Selective perception

Individuals differ in how they perceive the information in a message. This implies that people perceive messages based on their own individual perspectives or bias, with the result that two different people could interpret the same message very differently. This allows individuals to process and retain information that is contradictory to what they believe by changing their interpretation of the message.

Perhaps the best example of selective perception is the classic study by Albert Hastorf and Hadley Cantril in which students from Princeton and Dartmouth were asked to view a film of a rough game between the football teams of the two universities. Princeton students reported seeing twice as many rule infractions than reported by the Dartmouth students.[13] Hastorf and Cantril concluded that people interpret occurrences through the lens of their personal experiences, viewing events in a pattern that resonates with previous attitudes.

Consequences of selectivity

Individuals' selection behaviors can lead to a number of very different outcomes.

Polarization

There is evidence from the 2004 U.S. presidential election that a pattern of partisan selective exposure to news media increased the degree of polarization among voters over the course of the election.[14] Because messages that match previously held beliefs have a greater chance of being processed, selective exposure, attention, retention, and perception can be factors in the polarization of political attitudes. To use a current example, the initial step in this process could be that people who are critics of President Barack Obama choose to selectively expose themselves only to news media and information critical of the president. Similarly, they could choose to ignore information that is positive toward the president, while attending to negative information. Even if critics of the president are accidentally exposed to positive information, they could purge this from their memory and only retain the negative information. Finally, even if the critics of the president are exposed to some positive information, accidentally attend to and retain this information, they may still perceive the information to be negative. In this case, previously held negative attitudes toward President Obama would be reinforced by selective exposure, attention, retention, and perception. This reinforcement of previously held attitudes also could make individuals more and more polarized.

Hostile media effect

As Chapter 2's discussion of bias noted, individuals have a tendency to believe the news media have a bias against their beliefs and attitudes. They also believe the media get their side of stories wrong. Partisans see biases even when the news coverage is balanced, an outcome that results to a considerable degree from selective perception.

The most disheartening aspect of the hostile media effect is that the news media are in a lose-lose situation. The news media strive for balance in their news stories, providing all sides of political debates. News consumers, however, tend to only see the information in the stories that conflicts with their opinions.

Other opinions about the media

Although, as previously noted, the credibility of the news media has been declining for some time, nonetheless, the public has been satisfied with the performance of the media. A Pew Research Center survey after the 2000 U.S. presidential election found that 75 percent of the respondents reported they had learned enough about the candidates to make a choice and 62 percent said that media coverage of the debates was helpful. Despite this mixed picture, the news media may have an even more significant role in the future. Though newspaper readership is down, there also has been a steady decline in party identification among the public since 1952. With less emphasis on voting the party line, individuals will have a greater need for the political information that the news media provide.

Individual-level perspectives

There are a rich variety of perspectives on how individuals use, learn from, and are affected by mass media. In addition to those discussed in previous chapters, three additional perspectives are considered here.

Mira Sotirovic and Jack McLeod argue for an information-processing approach, which again assumes active processing by media consumers.[15] This perspective asserts that individuals actively collect, store, modify, interpret, and incorporate new information with what they already know about the world. This activity proceeds according to their goals, motives, and needs.

Individuals typically demonstrate stronger learning from newspapers than from television. These differences in learning rates could be due to the differences in form between print and broadcast. Print allows readers to process information at their own pace and to stop and reflect, which is not possible for television news viewers. The content of the two media also differ somewhat, with television concentrating more on candidates and newspapers focusing on political parties.

Wayne Wanta investigated public opinion formation from the perspective of the agenda-setting process. Using a path analysis model that identified four stages, he found that a number of demographic variables such as educational level and age led to political interest. In the second stage, political interest led to reliance on the news media for information. Next, reliance on the media led to both media use and interpersonal communication. Finally, media use and interpersonal communication led to susceptibility to media effects.[16]

The four stages of the model are logical. In the first stage, educational level was the strongest predictor of agenda-setting effects. Individuals with a high education level are best able to understand the significance of media content, and thus they should be most likely to show agenda-setting effects.

In the second stage, political interest was a strong predictor of agenda-setting effects. Again, the most interested individuals would be the most likely to be affected by news media content.

Next, reliance on news media for information is highly dependent upon political interest. The more interested in politics an individual is, the more they will become dependent upon the news media for information, as would be suggested by both uses and gratifications and media dependency theory.

Next, media reliance leads to media use. If individuals feel a high dependence on the news media, it is likely that they will use the media often.

Finally, exposure in tandem with interpersonal communication affects the magnitude of agenda-setting effects. Interpersonal communication can reinforce subsequent media exposure.

This model again demonstrates the active processing of information among individuals. Individuals with high education levels who are highly interested in politics, highly reliant on news media, and heavy consumers of news and interpersonal communication show the strongest agenda-setting effects.

Ran Wei and Ven Lo's cognitive mediation model also portrays the active processing of news content. During the 2006 midterm U.S. elections, motivation to use the media, exposure to the media, and attention to and elaboration of media content resulted in increased voter knowledge. Media exposure had direct and indirect effects on attention, elaboration, and knowledge about the election.[17]

Conclusion

Although the news media have substantial influence at each stage in the hierarchy of communication effects, this influence is far from monolithic. A wide variety of individual differences distinguishing one person from another also shapes the formation of public opinion. Demographics are the most familiar set of these individual characteristics. In terms of media use and its various civic outcomes, men and women differ, young adults and older adults differ, and those with college educations differ from those with less education. Individuals with different demographics interact with the media in very different ways.

In the very early days of communication research, audiences were largely viewed as passive recipients of the news and other media messages. However, by the 1940s what we now know as a uses and gratifications perspective began to appear in diverse studies: from why women listened to soap operas to what missing the newspaper means when strikes disrupt their publication. This active view of audiences came to the fore in the 1970s and 1980s, often merging with demographics as a major approach to the analysis of media use and its effects. For example, many senior citizens use the media for companionship and to overcome boredom, children tend to use media mainly for entertainment, and college students use media for guidance and to see the ideas and lifestyles of others.

This merger of these two perspectives is especially useful for understanding the audiences for the internet, with its highly diverse content. It must be noted, however, that these analyses are limited by the validity and completeness of self-reports and the clarity of the terms describing the gratifications sought and obtained from the internet.

One of oldest perspectives on individual differences in how

people process the news is grounded in the idea of selectivity: selective exposure to various media, selective attention to the content of those media, selective perception of the information in a message, and selective retention of that information over time. Major consequences of this selectivity include the political polarization of society, the hostile media effect, and the perceived credibility of the news media.

At a broader level, perspectives on how people learn from the news media include the information-processing, agenda-setting and social-learning, and cognitive mediation models. What is common to these three models and to all the other perspectives discussed here is the active participation by citizens in the political communication process. What citizens bring to the news is vitally important for understanding the influence of that news on the formation of public opinion.

11

News Influence on Civic Life

The news media have a central role in the formation of public opinion, and also facilitate the expression of public opinion in numerous ways. To gain an overview of these relationships between the news media and public opinion, the preceding chapters have systematically examined in detail the empirical social-science evidence regarding the sequence of outcomes that describe the formation and expression of public opinion. This sequence of outcomes, often referred to as the "hierarchy of media effects," extends from simple exposure to the news media to overt civic behavior such as going to the polls and casting a vote on Election Day. Now that we have completed our survey of this sequence step by step, our goal is to bring these outcomes together in an integrated picture of the political communication process. Understanding each component of this process is vital for both citizens and professional communicators. Even more vital is a comprehensive understanding of how all these components fit together.

To gain this comprehensive understanding, we begin at ground zero: each person's direct experience with the news media. For this experience there are important distinctions to be made between media exposure, media attention, and media use. Media *exposure* is literally that, physical exposure to a news outlet. This experience can range from purely incidental exposure—simply being in a place where a television news program is on or glimpsing bits of news from your internet provider's home page—to habitual exposure—reading the newspaper during breakfast, checking for news updates through a cellular phone, or purposely turning to a particular TV network's evening news program.

Even in the case of habitual behavior—deliberate efforts to be exposed to the news—there can be widely varying levels of *attention*. Some people turn on the TV news and pay close attention. Others simultaneously take up a second task, sometimes reading the newspaper or looking at a magazine, and pay only peripheral attention to the flow of news on the TV.

During both exposure and attention, there are vast individual differences in people's *experience* with the news media. Some people are exposed to the news many times a day. And they may pay considerable attention or only casual attention. At the other extreme, some people avoid the news as much as possible. Taking these individual differences into account becomes even more important for understanding variations in the uses and gratifications that are the psychological foundation for people's interactions with the news media. Two individuals may be highly attentive to the same political debate on TV. But one perceives it in terms of political conflict and the other as a source of information about the personalities and issue positions of the candidates. There can be the same exposure and level of attention, but very different experiences in terms of use. As a result, we cannot really talk about the news audience; we must talk about many different news audiences populated by a variety of subgroups that are defined by many different individual experiences.

We also need to abandon the idea of the various news media competing in a zero-sum game with one another for the attention of the public. Instead, we need to focus on how one type of news media experience serves to complement other types of news media experiences. One unequivocal empirical fact of long standing is that most individuals engage multiple information outlets in a variety of ways.

From this starting point—each individual's personal experience with the news media—we will review a set of key questions about the sequence of outcomes that can result from these experiences, always keeping in mind the range of individual differences as well as the aggregations of outcomes that define the ever-moving process of public opinion in society.

To *what extent do the news media make citizens aware of current public affairs?*

The news media are by far the most-used source for most of the information that each of us has about public affairs. The opening chapter of Walter Lippmann's classic *Public Opinion* is titled "The World Outside and the Pictures in Our Heads."[1] His thesis is that the news media are the key link between the world outside and our individual pictures of that world. Most important, both the stream of news reports and our mental pictures are a highly truncated version of the vast world outside. In part because of the necessity of constructing a highly edited version of what is happening in the world, the news media do more than contribute the bits and pieces of information that we use to construct our mental pictures. Their pattern of news coverage focuses our attention on particular aspects of the world and provides a set of cues about what has priority status.

As a result, when pollsters ask citizens what they think is the most important problem facing the country at the moment, the aggregate set of responses closely mirrors the pattern of news coverage over recent days and weeks. That is, the rank-order of the issues of the day based on the amount of news coverage corresponds very closely to the rank-order of the issues found in the public's aggregate response to the pollster's question. This influence of the media on the focus of public attention is called the agenda-setting role of the news media, an influence that has been documented for a wide range of public issues as well as other public-affairs topics, over many decades and in countries on every continent.

This agenda-setting influence of the news media extends beyond focusing public attention on particular issues or other political objects. When the news media discuss an issue or public figure or other political object, they also describe some aspects of that object. Some of these attributes of the object are emphasized, others mentioned from time to time, some only in passing, and many not at all. Just as the issues or other objects on the media agenda and the public agenda can be rank-ordered, the attributes of each object on the media and public agendas also can be rank-ordered. And, again, a high degree of correspondence has been found between the media and public across a wide variety of public affairs settings. The news media influence what our pictures of the world outside are about as well as literally what our pictures are. This is a powerful role for media in the formation of public opinion.

Does the news make citizens appropriately knowledgeable about politics?

Learning from the news media also depends on two other distinct sets of factors: individual differences among citizens, and the style of news reports and programs that present public-affairs information. Both of these factors influence how much individual citizens learn from the news and what kinds of information they acquire.

Motivation is a consistent factor in the acquisition of civic knowledge. The motivations that drive exposure and attention to the news range from very general motivations (such as a sense of civic duty) to very specific motivations described by the psychological uses and gratifications linked to particular topics. Education also is important and creates uneven knowledge gains, even with similar levels of media experience. Individuals with high levels of education typically learn from the media at a faster rate than individuals with low education levels.

Another consistent finding is that newspaper readers learn more than television viewers. With the increased reliance on the internet, this factor could be double-edged. On the one hand, the print versions of newspapers continue to lose readership. On the other hand, internet versions of newspapers are flourishing. These distinctions among media channels become more blurred when we consider the accessibility of news and public-affairs information through mobile devices and other forms of digital communication. With the contemporary proliferation of media channels, individual differences in exposure, attention, and the uses and gratifications of the types and amounts of news seen by citizens play a key role in what is acquired from the news. There also is a vast difference between the rather gray pages of most daily newspapers and the shouting matches of some cable TV programs, with the presentation of much other civic information somewhere in the middle.

Most important, exactly what is learned from the news media? For most citizens the acquisition of public affairs information is a casual process, sometimes even incidental, and their knowledge of public affairs accumulates incrementally over long periods of time. Michael Schudson posits a monitorial citizen, who for the most part casually monitors the news until something of particular relevance appears on his or her personal radar.[2] Samuel Popkin describes the variety of mental shortcuts that large numbers of citizens use in making ballot decisions.[3] And Anthony Downs pessimistically argues that citizens have little incentive to engage in complex patterns of learning because each person has only a single vote.[4] Although all of these perspectives suggest that the typical citizen is a rather casual student of public affairs who would have difficulty with any comprehensive examination of their civic knowledge, nevertheless, the aggregate outcome is not necessarily dismal.

Do *the news media contribute to stable opinions and attitudes?*

An extensive analysis of 50 years of public opinion trends by Benjamin Page and Robert Shapiro concluded that in the aggregate the public does reach very rational decisions about the issues of the day.[5] Their conclusion supports a basic democratic assumption about the collective wisdom of the people. By inference, it underscores the important civic contribution of the news media.

Historically, this contribution at times has been disdained and regarded as minimal or even non-existent because of a narrow focus on the influence of the news media in changing attitudes and opinions. In recent decades, however, researchers have realized that opinion formation and reinforcement can be just as important a set of outcomes as opinion change when considering the consequences of news.

The extent to which the public in the aggregate has any opinion at all about a public issue or political candidate is strongly linked to patterns of news coverage. Even at the end of the lengthy U.S. presidential campaign, there remains a modest percentage of Americans who still have no opinions about the Democrat and Republican candidates, and the size of this percentage fluctuates inversely with the amount of news coverage over the months of the campaign. The greater the amount of news about the presidential campaign, the smaller the percentage of people who fail to form an opinion about the candidates. Thus, the extent to which the news activates opinions about candidates has the potential to determine election outcomes, especially in close races.

Extensive news coverage can prime certain issues as the criteria that individuals use when they are asked their opinion about the performance of the president. This is a direct connection between patterns of news coverage and public opinion. Details of the news coverage on issues and political candidates also are related to public opinion about these political objects. The salience of the attributes of these issues or candidates in the news—and especially the affective dimension of these attributes—is related to the images that citizens have about these issues and candidates as well as the opinions the public holds about them.

Especially in the case of opinions, the accumulated tone of news coverage plays a key role. Our tendency to emphasize a rational-person model of political communication among the public needs to be complemented with an emotional-person model of political communication. Emotions, especially negative ones such as fear and anger, affect the public's response to a variety of issues and affect the public's images and opinions of political candidates and political parties. Both the substance of the news and the tone of the news have major implications for the formation and expression of public opinion.

Does the news lead to opinions about a wider variety of political topics?

Just as the news has a profound effect on the degree to which a citizen is aware of political issues, so too the news media also influence the range of issues on which people hold opinions. Each citizen can deal with only a rather small range of public issues on any given day. A senior citizen may focus on Social Security and Medicare. A college student might be concerned with student loan policies, education reform issues, or perhaps issues related to reproductive rights. A doctor or nurse may be especially attentive to healthcare issues. People do, however, hold opinions about a much broader range of issues than those made salient to them through their day-to-day activities and immediate personal interests.

This additional breadth of opinion most certainly can stem from various interpersonal engagements, either face-to-face or through some form of computer-mediated communication. The ability of these forms of communication to expand the breadth of opinion is rather limited, however, when compared to media's potential influence. The people you most often come into contact with on a daily basis are dealing with many of the same issues as you, so the ability of these face-to-face encounters to truly expand the breadth of opinion formation is limited in comparison to the potential of the mass media.

It is important to look at this media influence in a more complex fashion, however, extending our discussion to encompass both direct and indirect effects. First, the direct effects: we need to look no further than the opinions we hold about a range of international issues. Without the news media, citizens would not be aware of many issues taking place abroad. And we are not only aware of issues taking shape in other countries; we have an opportunity to gain enough information to form an opinion about these international issues. An American citizen may have an opinion about a separatist movement in Spain, a trade issue between Russia and the European Union, or the treatment of immigrant populations in New Zealand or Australia. Despite the lack of any direct experience with these issues or any face-to-face contact with anyone else who has a personal stake in these issues, the news media provide enough details about these matters to enable one to form an opinion.

In terms of indirect effects, let's return to the influence of inter-personal communication on a citizen's breadth of opinions. Very frequently the source of information for an individual who is communicating an opinion to another citizen is the news media. Thus, the news media can have an indirect effect on the breadth of opinion formation through its impact on interpersonal political discussion. This point serves to reemphasize the need to study how various forms of communication work in coordination with one another to produce a range of democratic outcomes. For the most part, mass communication and interpersonal communication serve to complement one another.

Does the news lead to increased political participation?

There is a clear and consistent relationship between news use and various forms of political participation, both conventional (volunteering for a campaign or voting, say) or unconventional (for instance, taking part in a civic forum or writing a political blog entry). The strength of this association is not as strong as one would assume, however, and is not anywhere near the strength of the effects of news use on the levels of awareness generated about specific issues. In general, news media influence is stronger for the earlier stages of the hierarchy of effects, with smaller effect sizes found as one migrates through the hierarchy to overt behaviors.

Additional points of qualification are required in explaining the relationship between news media use and various types of political participation. First, the strength of the associations between news media use and political behaviors varies by medium. Stronger associations have been found when newspaper use has been iso-lated from other forms of traditional news use, while the strength of this relationship is much weaker for television. In terms of new media, the general consensus is that the use of news media via the internet produces associations with various types of political behavioral engagement that are on par with newspaper use.

The comparison of new and old news media use relative to political behaviors needs further qualification. These relationships are highly dependent upon individual differences. For example, a classic distinction concerning consumption of print-based news about public affairs is the age of the people engaged in this activity. In contrast, many of the political and civic effects of new media are found in younger generations. Isolation of this cohort reveals much stronger associations between new media-oriented news consumption and political participation. In short, it is important to look at the relationship between news media use and a broad range of political behaviors in the context of individual differences that can influence the use of particular media and subsequent engagement in various types of civic activity.

The distinction between conventional and nonconventional forms of political participation brings up a parallel issue. Not all forms of engagement that are important to a well-functioning democracy are inherently political. A broad range of activities that are not inspired by politics or even directly related to politics affects the day-to-day functioning of a democracy. These nonpolitical activities can foster social capital, a resource that exists as a result of a mutually reinforcing relationship between interpersonal trust and civic activity. Adequate levels of social capital are arguably a necessary, but not sufficient, condition for a well-functioning democracy. Although the relationship between news media use and the various attitudinal and behavioral elements defining social capital has not been found to be strong, it is also important to note that the contrary conclusion argued by some—that media have a detrimental effect on social capital—clearly has not been shown to be the case.

Do *the news media polarize the electorate?*

The issue of polarization is of central importance given the present state of American politics. A central question is the degree to which journalism (how it presents politics and public affairs) affects the polarization of the public. This question becomes more complex as we consider the intricate set of relationships that exist among news media organizations, elites, and the general population.

It is not simply the case that the messages provided by news organizations have become more polarized, and that this has created greater polarization within the audience. We need to step far beyond this simple type of stimulus-response model. One possible explanation for polarization is grounded in the concept of selective exposure, which dates from the earliest days of communication research. It has been argued that citizens have a natural tendency to gravitate toward messages that reinforce or generally reflect their pre-existing worldview, and furthermore that citizens tend to shy away from media outlets which run counter to their pre-existing worldviews. Serious concerns have been raised about whether the latter of these two assumptions is correct, however, and recent research indicates that a preference for congenial media content does not necessarily lead to the avoidance of contrary views.[6]

A second point that has been raised by Lance Bennett and Shanto Iyengar is the changing nature of the news media land-scape.[7] There is no question that with the tremendous expansion in the number of television channels and the rise of the internet as a vast source for news, audience members now have the ability to gain access to news content which suits any particular ideological bent. Any conclusions about whether news media are producing greater polarization among citizens, however, will depend on how you define "news." Schudson has identified three distinct models of journalism: the market, advocacy, and trustee models.[8] Should we include all three models in our consideration of the role of news media in the polarization of the electorate? Do news organizations who have long embraced the trustee model contribute to greater polarization? We would argue that these news organizations have not done so. Can the same be said, however, for organizations that embrace an advocacy model? We would argue that the same conclusion cannot be reached for advocacy-oriented outlets. In short, the model of journalism that defines a news organization serves as an important moderator in any discussion of the role of news media and political polarization.

Does the news disenfranchise some citizens and create participation gaps?

There are knowledge gaps in society because citizens who are higher in socioeconomic status tend to gain more knowledge about a new issue from the media over time, leading to even greater differentials in political knowledge than the already sizeable distinctions between high and low socioeconomic citizen status that exist generally. An indirect effect of the creation of a knowledge gap would be formation of participation gaps, if we assume that political knowledge influences political behaviors.

The changing media landscape is also an important factor in the creation of political participation gaps. The size of the news audience is shrinking. More people who do not wish to come into contact with the news now have more than enough viable media options to allow them to forgo news consumption altogether. As a result, there is a potential for news media to produce ever-widening behavior gaps between those who consume a great deal of news, which the rise of the new media landscape also allows, and an increasingly larger segment of the population who detach themselves from news altogether.

Another important concept related to news media and participation gaps is what Paul Lazarsfeld and Robert Merton defined a half century ago as the narcotizing dysfunction of news media consumption.[9] The basic idea is that news media offer audience members a true flood of information on just about any topic related to politics and public affairs, and the consumption of this news content can make someone feel as though they are engaged in the political process when in fact there is little actual behavioral engagement. This flow of information can narcotize or lull someone into thinking they are politically engaged when in fact they are not. It is not simply the consumption of news versus the lack of consumption that produces political participation gaps. There is clearly the potential that among some citizens large volumes of news media can actually create a barrier that serves to hinder political participation.

Do the news media influence policymaking?

Policymakers, issue advocates, and all other elites who are involved in the formation, alteration, and debating of public policy are engaged continuously with the news media. These members of the political elite do so because they know that news media shape the public policy process in important ways.

Anthony Downs outlined a sequence that intricately involves news media, showing how topics of public policy gain and lose citizens' attention over time.[10] This five-step process, called the issue attention cycle, begins with the pre-problem stage. This name is somewhat misleading because the stage does not reflect the lack of a public problem, but only the lack of *awareness* on the part of the public about this problem. The second stage is the "alarmed discovery and euphoric enthusiasm" phase in which some specific event or situation brings a problem to light in rather dramatic fashion. In the third stage the public begins to come to terms with the size of the problem, its relative importance, and what it is going to take to resolve the problem in terms of time, human resources, and money. At this point in the process, problems that generate significant levels of cognitive dissonance or where the importance does not outweigh the cost lose attention rather quickly. This brings on the fourth stage, a gradual decline in the intensity of a citizen's engagement with the problem. The final stage is defined by Downs as "a prolonged limbo" where public interest has waned sufficiently so that rival public policy problems take the former issue's place in terms of being highly salient for the public. Of course, once another issue arises, the same five-stage issue cycle begins again with a new ebb and flow in public attentiveness.

In terms of the role of news in this issue-attention cycle, it is clear that journalism can particularly influence how, when, and why various issues reach the alarmed discovery stage. In many cases, it is the news coverage of an issue originated by the media that creates alarmed discovery among the general public. And even in situations where events themselves or the actions of other political actors generate the news coverage, the nature of that coverage can enhance the breadth and the depth of the alarm and euphoria among the public that is becoming aware of a particular issue. The framing of the issue will also influence how members of the public come to understand the following aspects of it: the scope of the problem, who is affected, how central the problem is to the functioning of society, what the potential solutions are to the problem, and, often most important, what the costs will be to fix the problem. News coverage also can help determine how long each stage of the issue cycle endures before cycling to the next stage to the next. For example, the intensity of news coverage on an issue can affect the rate of decline in the public's interest and when, or even if, the issue settles back into a post-problem phase.

Conclusion

The broad range of news media effects on democratic life can be classified according to a number of different dichotomies.[11] Keeping these dichotomies in mind allows us to see a broader picture of what we have been able to understand to date, what we still need to understand better, and what we can offer in terms of some better predictions about the future. In addition, these dichotomies will serve as an especially important foundation when we consider normative evaluations of the news media's job performance in the concluding chapter.

An especially important distinction when thinking about any news media effect is whether the effect is intended or unintended. A classic intended effect of the news is fostering political knowledge. It clearly is the intention of individual journalists and trustee-oriented news organizations to supply the public with information that enhances their knowledge and understanding of an issue. Whether the information provided is accurate or inaccurate, and even whether it is the primary intention of individual journalists or news organizations to provide accurate or inaccurate information, is another issue entirely.

On the other hand, unintended effects raised in our discussion of media effects are the creation of knowledge and political participation gaps. It is generally not the intention of news organizations to create greater disadvantages for those who are lower in socioeconomic status, but there is a solid foundation of empirical research documenting that the consumption of news across time by these distinct subpopulations can generate both types of gaps.

Another important distinction is whether the media effects are direct or indirect. A classic distinction between a direct and an indirect effect can be found in the evolution of the research on agenda setting. The classic agenda-setting hypothesis of a transfer of salience from the media to the public is a reflection of a direct effect. Recent work by Spiro Kiousis and Maxwell McCombs, however, suggests that the direct relationship between media salience and public salience may be mediated, at least under some conditions, by attitude strength.[12] Under these circumstances, the news media's influence on public salience is no longer direct but indirect. It is important to expand our understanding of news media effects beyond direct effects as we try to make more global judgments about the role of news media in democratic life. The study of communication is the study of process. To examine only those news media effects which are direct, while ignoring the range of indirect effects, would result in substantially underestimating the influence of news.

Another important distinction is whether media effects stem from content or form. There are many instances in the previous chapters which show how the actual messages offered by news media influence a range of democratic outcomes. Indeed, it is natural to think about content effects when envisioning the role of media in producing a range of democratic outcomes. There also is the potential for form-generated effects, however. Introduction of a new medium has the potential to affect democracy in ways quite separate from the news provided through that medium. Many of the discussions about the role of new media in democracy center on issues of form, not content. Some scholars believe that all the important effects of media can be traced back to content, while others (although a relative minority) feel that the only meaningful effects of media stem from form, not content. Most scholars, however, embrace the notion that a broad range of news media effects stem from a mix of content and form.

Now, building on our understanding of media effects on public opinion, we turn in the final chapter to a normative assessment of the news media's positive and negative contributions.

III

Coming to Judgment

12

Assessing the Role of News in Civic Life

The news media have significant effects on individuals' civic life and the way that the democratic process actually works in practice. Now it is important to move from the empirical to the normative. Are these effects good or bad? Do they enhance or do they constrain, even distort or derail, a robust civic life? And even in those cases where the contribution of the news media is judged to be positive, is that contribution as strong and comprehensive as it could be? Social scientists can answer our questions about what the contributions of the news media are. Journalists and citizens should focus on questions about what the contributions of the news media should be in order to facilitate a thriving democracy.

This final chapter is an opening gambit in a continuing conversation about civic life. Revisiting the same series of questions posed in the previous chapter to summarize the effects of the news media, the focus here will be on a normative assessment of how well the news media are doing in these important areas of civic life. Among the questions central to this discussion are the following:

- Are the news media sufficiently free from the influence of specific interests to function as independent social institutions who monitor our political and social environment?
- Is the breadth and depth of the news sufficient and presented in a manner that is relevant to the needs and interests of the diverse subpopulations for public affairs news? As metaphorically described by Lester Milbrath, these subpublics range

from actively involved gladiators to the spectators who cheer and jeer the spectacle and decide on the Election Day victors.[1]

- Related to the needs and interests of the various publics for the news is a key question stimulated by the new media landscape about the appropriate relationships—even partnerships— among citizens, the news media, and policymakers.

These questions are grounded in the themes that will be discussed here in our normative assessment of the impact that the news media have on the elements of civic life.

To *what extent do the news media make citizens aware of current public affairs?*

There is strong evidence that the news media generate awareness among the public about a variety of important public issues. A central question here, however, is the degree to which news media organizations are independent agencies in determining which issues are given more versus less attention. Journalists use a variety of sources to gain an understanding of the major issues of the day, and each source brings an agenda concerning which issues should be deemed important and worthy of coverage. In making their determinations about what becomes part of "the news" on any given day, do news organizations make these decisions free from the influence of these sources? And are the various factions involved in any public issue afforded equal treatment?

It is difficult to make global judgments about the state of news regarding these queries given the present diversity of news organizations and the rise of the web as a source for political and public policy information. Looking at America's largest and most respected news organizations, such as *The New York Times*, *Washington Post*, *Wall Street Journal*, and the major network television news divisions, there is general agreement that these organizations retain at least a moderate degree of independence from other elite institutions, particularly the three major branches of the federal government. Concerns have been voiced about news organizations inherent ties to large corporations, however—for example, NBC and General Electric—now that media have become big business.[2] To what degree do corporate interests affect what is or is not being covered as "news"?

Beyond these major news organizations, concerns also have been voiced about ties between news organizations and the political establishment. The best-known example of this phenomenon is cable television's Fox News. There is clear evidence of Fox News' strong ties to America's conservative Republican Party. Much of the agenda put forward by Fox News about which issues of the day should be covered are those emphasized by the Republican Party.[3]

The rise of digital media also raises questions about the degree to which news organizations "appropriately" make citizens aware of the major issues of the day. Digital media is reflective of infinite space, and this space needs to be filled up with content. As a result, many, many more issues can be covered, and it is especially important to consider whether many of the issues being raised by news organizations are worthy of the public's attention.

With all these caveats in mind, a solid case can be made that a vast majority of news organizations exercise a fair degree of independence from those elite institutions for which they are watchdogs. In addition, most news organizations also take their role of gatekeeper seriously, and there remain in place solid decision-making processes that serve to bring to light those issues that are of greatest importance to a vast majority of the citizenry. There are news organizations that do not fit this general description, however, and there are also instances when journalistic practice does fall short of this standard. One example would be the lack of significant news coverage of the unsound financial and banking practices leading up to the global financial crises of 2008–2009.

Does the news make citizens appropriately knowledgeable about politics?

There is a positive relationship between exposure to the news and knowledge about politics and public affairs. Because the size of this media effect is relatively small, however, much remains to be done by news organizations. In particular, the news media can do a far better job of supplying people with the type of information they need to be more engaged citizens.

What type of knowledge should we focus on in thinking about what best aids citizens in their various democratic activities? Is it basic civics knowledge—for example, who is the current vice president of the United States—or basic political process questions—When is Election Day this year?—or a broader set of questions that speak to becoming involved in a community—How do you go about forming a petition? Do people need all of these different types of information in order to be well-functioning citizens? Which types of information are more important and what types are less so? And most important, which types of information are most effectively conveyed by news media?

These important questions are key elements in the public journalism movement and other likeminded attempts in the last two decades to rethink how journalists should approach their role in democratic society.[4] Public journalists made the case that journalists need to do a better job of stepping into the shoes of citizens and asking themselves what information people need in order to become more civically engaged. A broader argument made by public journalists was that one significant reason why the general news audience was shrinking is the fact that newspapers, television news, and other sources of public affairs information were not giving people all the information they desired and needed in order to be good citizens. In particular, the news media are highly efficient at making people aware of the key issues of the day, but far less efficient in systematically reporting the various aspects of an issue and the details of proposed solutions. With this being said, questions also were raised about whether news organizations can retain an adequate level of independence from the larger social fabric if they actively seek to cajole the public into becoming more involved in daily civic activities.[5] Regardless of where one ultimately stands on this issue, suffice it to say that these basic normative concerns remain a vibrant part of the discussion about the state of journalism.

Trust in news media also must be a part of any discussion about whether news organizations assist citizens to become "appropriately knowledgeable" about politics. Even when the news media supply all the information needed for citizens to become properly engaged in civic life, if members of the general public do not trust these news organizations, then the news will have much weaker effects. Trust in news media is at an all-time low at the moment, and there is a clear need for the news media to re-establish a sense of trust within the general public in order to fulfill their civic responsibility.

Do *the news media contribute to stable opinions and attitudes?*

The relationship between exposure to the news and political attitudes and opinions consists of far more than just persuasion and attitude change. In considering the effects of the news, it is essential to think about the degree to which the continuous stream of news reports seen by most citizens aids in the formation, modification, and strengthening of opinions across time, not just the degree to which news has the ability to create fundamental changes in opinions about a political candidate or public issue.

The issue of creation and strengthening versus the outright change of an attitude or opinion is of particular interest with the rise of new media and the way in which citizens can now come into contact with news. The "push" versus "pull" media environments that symbolize old versus new media create unique distinctions when one thinks about the relationship between use of the news media and citizens' political attitudes. Push media represent the classic conceptualization of mass media—one-way, top-down communication where elites make decisions about what content will be offered and when, with very little direct feedback from the audience. In contrast, pull media reflect a two-way communicative process, initiated in large part by the audience member and characterized by a certain amount of provinciality—"this is what I have always attended to." Surprise and incidental exposure to new topics, however, may arguably be an important contribution of the news to civic life.

There is no question that a strong set of opinions and attitudes is often essential to being politically engaged. However, can strong and stable individual attitudes and opinions result from rational discourse? Lance Bennett and Shanto Iyengar argue that we are witnessing a rise in strong, more partisan opinions, and that the news media, which are becoming increasingly partisan, are strengthening these views by providing a largely irrational civic discourse.[6] Robert Holbert and his associates point out, however, that as individuals' opinions become stronger they are more likely to feel confident enough to seek out alternative points of view, at least for the purpose of knowing what needs to be refuted.[7] This is an inherently complex picture that we must continue to examine.

Does the news lead to opinions about a wider variety of political topics?

The issue of what is an impression versus an opinion needs to be considered because exposure to the news allows individuals to form impressions about a far wider range of topics than they might otherwise do during the course of their daily routine. How many of these impressions are sufficiently detailed or strong to be defined as opinions? To what extent do the news media foster the creation of opinions in contrast to fleeting impressions?

News media often provide the types of information that would allow for the forming of opinions. Much of the process of opinion formation, however, exists outside the influence of news organizations. It is up to individuals to take the information they gain from the news, perhaps utilize it in conversations, and then take the time to reflect in order to establish their own opinions. The opinion formation process involves many steps, only one of which involves the consumption of news. It is frequently the case, however, that news consumption is a central step in the process, so central that the rest of the process does not take shape without news exposure. And because exposure to the news is so crucial to the process of opinion formation, it is incumbent upon news organizations to provide a detailed account of all the major issues of the day, to supply the news relevant to citizenship and democratic governance, not just those news stories with dramatic headlines appealing to citizens' curiosity.

Does the news lead to increased political participation?

Although there is a significant correlation between news use and participation in civic life, the strength of this relationship is far from overwhelming. The links between use of the news media and effects among citizens grow progressively weaker as we move along the hierarchy of effects. Whereas the agenda-setting effects of the news media on the public's perceptions of the major issues of the day are strong, the effects of the news media on observable behavior are modest. This is ironic given the long-standing exhortation of almost every newspaper's editorial page on Election Day to go to the polls and vote.

Part of the explanation for this declining impact of the news media on successive stages of the hierarchy of effects is the growing number of additional factors that are involved in each successive effect. What we see in the news is a major factor in our assessment of which issues of the day are important. What we see in the news is only a small factor in the set of variables that determine our participation in various civic activities. What also is missing here on the part of the news media, however, is systematic attention to the full array of details that define the major issues of the day. The state of the economy, healthcare, public education, or engagement in Iraq and Afghanistan, to name four issues that have been at the top of the issue agenda in recent years, are very complex issues with numerous facets. How complete a picture does the public receive of these issues? All too often the major attention is directed at the political skirmishing over these issues, the equivalent of the "horse-race" coverage that has been vigorously criticized in presidential election campaigns.[8]

Pioneer political communication scholar Harold Lasswell noted that the three major functions of mass communication are surveillance, creation of consensus, and communication of cultural norms.[9] There is no question that the news media perform an important surveillance function, but how thorough is that performance? The existence of fairly strong agenda-setting effects speaks directly to the creation of consensus. But what about the communication of cultural norms, especially regarding citizenship? Individuals' sense of civic duty is directly linked to their frequency of exposure to the news media. But is this sense of duty fostered by the media themselves? Or does the heavy dose of negative and cynical coverage of politics in the news foster higher degrees of cynicism among many members of the public?

On the positive side of the ledger, the proliferation of news media on the web—a channel with low entry costs relative to newspapers and television and with infinitely larger capacities—affords an opportunity for a closer relationship between news coverage and the varied information needs of individual citizens. This is especially the case in regard to civic and political participation at the local level. Citizen journalism, where citizens themselves, rather than professional journalists, draft—if not totally present—many news reports is proliferating at the community level. And web servers for neighborhood associations and some news media have the capacity for this "long tail" model of news reports, a model in which there are a large number of niche items each appealing to only a small segment of the public. This is a model that seems likely to stimulate greater levels of participation, or at least offers a wider array of possibilities by which news media can influence greater engagement in politics. These trends also may offer alternative business models for journalism, given the dramatic economic constraints affecting the news media in recent years.

Do *the news media polarize the electorate?*

In a push-dominated media environment, conditions are less than optimal for the news media to shape attitudes and opinions, whereas in the pull media environment citizen motivation and ability levels (key elements that determine the potential for significant attitude change) are much more likely to be optimized. A key question regarding pull media is the degree to which citizens will only seek out those news media that largely reinforce their pre-existing political worldviews.[10] There is some recent empirical evidence that citizens do not actively avoid those outlets that run counter to their established political orientations.[11] Needless to say, more evidence is needed before definitive judgments can be made.

Most important, there is the broader question of how strong and stable we want citizens' attitudes and opinions to be. Stability can speak to the potential for rigidity.

Initially, this question brings to mind the advocacy model of journalism, an approach to the news in which particular political positions on the issues of the day are emphasized. A troubling aspect here is the degree to which they clearly identify their political predilection versus portraying themselves as nonpartisan presenters of news who are above the political fray. Among the advocates, the opinion magazines get the highest marks for their transparency. *The Nation, The New Republic, The National Review,* and their peers are quite open about their political predilection while cable TV's Fox News, for example, is less transparent about its political orientation.

In the contemporary news landscape some of the news organizations adhering to an advocacy model also have an editorial strategy that includes sensationalism. One must question what contribution sensationalistic advocacy really makes to our political dialogue and to serious deliberation on the complexities of the issues of the day. Of course, sensationalism and advocacy are not necessarily coupled. There are any number of news outlets that clearly favor a conservative or liberal agenda, but do so in articles characterized by serious expository writing rather than sensationalistic presentation.

Discussion of polarization effects of the news on the public cannot be limited to the advocacy model, but must also include the trustee model that dominated mainstream news for the last half of the twentieth century, a model of journalism focused on public service and the presentation of information rather than commentary. Even in this intellectual setting there are important normative questions about how to implement this role in day-to-day reporting about government and public issues. At the extreme, objectivity means the careful and accurate reporting of the actions and statements of public officials, a stance that can reduce journalists to the role of stenographers. In reaction, the reporting of presidential campaigns, for example, became more and more interpretative during the final decades of the twentieth century. But at what point does interpretation shade into advocacy and serve one portion of the political spectrum more than another?

Whichever model is followed, it is important to recognize that the news is a sample of the events and perspectives of the day regarding public affairs, a sample that is based on news values that at times overvalue the dramatic and emotional. The potential for this approach to the news to arouse strong feelings and sharply divide the public is a significant ethical issue.

Finally, the market role might appear to be the least relevant for political communication because it implies a business model in which news organizations seek to maximize their market with news stories that draw wide attention among the public and provide instant gratification. These generally are stories that satisfy our curiosity about the world more than our need to understand the world. However, this inattention to public affairs—or attention to only its more sensational aspects—can have the effect of further reducing the salience of public life among many members of the public. Citizens holding strong opinions are more likely to participate in public life, and the amount of coverage on an issue, election, or other public matter is highly correlated with the proportion of the public who hold any opinion at all.

Does the news disenfranchise some citizens and create participation gaps?

The strong relationship between the amount of news coverage on a topic and the proportion of the public holding strong opinions about that matter is highly encouraging, suggesting a strategy for reducing knowledge and participation gaps. Comprehensive, continuing coverage of the key issues of the day can make people aware, build their store of knowledge, assist in the formation of their opinions, and stimulate their civic participation. In short, a focused strategy of news coverage can make at least some aspects of public affairs relevant to virtually everyone.

Half a century ago, the Hutchins Commission elaborated a normative set of criteria for news coverage of public affairs, criteria that offer tactical guidance to the news media for organizing their news coverage of public affairs in a way that can make that coverage relevant across a highly diverse citizenry.[12] Foremost among these criteria are providing a truthful, comprehensive, and intelligent account of each day's events in a context that brings out their full meaning; and providing a representative picture of the various social groups that constitute American society.

Public issues typically are complex and not every facet of every issue is relevant with every citizen. Coverage across the multiple aspects of each issue is likely to result in some portion of the issue resonating with a subpublic for whom that aspect of the issue is deemed relevant. Establishing a meaningful relationship between news coverage and the perceived relevance by citizens for at least some portion of that coverage is likely to be facilitated when members of various subpublics, especially minority groups and those with lower levels of education and income, find people like themselves in the news.

The relevance of the public issues of the day is perceived from two perspectives: the social relevance of an issue—its impact and meaning for the larger society—and the personal relevance of an issue—its impact and meaning for an individual's situation. It is the responsibility of the news media to make both of these connections in their news coverage, which is to say, it is their responsibility to communicate—in the full sense of that word—with the public about the issues of the day. Knowledge gaps and participation gaps among various groups in society shrink as issues become more relevant to all.

Finally, we must make an important note on a major by-product of intensive, comprehensive coverage of the issues of the day. Although many persons may use both the traditional media and the panoply of new media primarily as a source of entertainment rather than for seeking out information about public affairs, few can avoid some exposure to the news. And this incidental exposure to the news has significant impact across the hierarchy of media effects. Although these effects may not be as powerful as those resulting from greater levels of attention, nevertheless, they are present and contribute to the process of democracy.

Does news media use influence policymaking?

There is clearly an argument to be made that news media can shape the breadth and depth of public policy issues being discussed by political elites. James Ettema makes a strong case that the influence of news on policymaking can be felt in its effects on elite-to-elite relationships.[13] There is also a need to recognize that the influence of the news on policymaking processes can be seen through its effects among the broader citizenry.

In past decades of mass communication where daily newspapers and TV news dominated which issues were at the top of the news agenda, that agenda in turn largely dominated the public's attention. Now as we move into a new media landscape characterized by interactivity, there are numerous signs predicting more of a partnership between the three pillars of democracy—the government, the public, and the news media—in determining the news agenda, the public's focus of attention, and the formation of public policy regarding the key issues of the day. We hear a wide range of voices advocating increased interaction between citizens and the news media in the shaping of the news agenda, as well as advocating increased interaction between citizens and the government in the shaping of public policy.

There also are signs of new partnerships that have explicit, observable outcomes on the news agenda and on the policy agenda. At first glance, much of this activity appears to be limited to episodic outcroppings of interactive partnerships. However, looking back a dozen years or more reveals an evolving institutionalized pattern of increased interactivity. Historically, this is grounded in the century-old debate between Walter Lippmann and John Dewey and their acolytes about the civic role of individual citizens. The more recent foundation of a stronger media–public partnership was the rise of civic journalism in the 1990s. This perspective advocated a news agenda less dominated by elites and more inclusive of citizens' voices and their concerns, and also advocated the facilitation of public deliberation about the potential solutions for the major problems of the day. Viewed by some as an advocacy model for the news, it is more appropriately viewed as an expanded version of the trustee model. Although the terms "civic journalism" or "public journalism" are less frequently heard today, this perspective has influenced the day-to-day practice of journalism. There is a growing body of evidence, for example, that citizens' concerns and perspectives now appear more frequently in the news along with more discussion of potential solutions to problems. And most important, there is evidence that exposure to this expanded news agenda has an impact on knowledge, attitudes, and behavior. Politicians and public officials have long regarded news accounts as a measure of public opinion, which means that an expanded representation of the public in the news exerts an indirect but significant influence on the shaping of policy.

This influence of the public is likely to expand as citizen journalism becomes more widespread. Some journalists regard the interaction between news organizations and citizens as essentially a feedback process in which citizens react to the stories presented to them, perhaps offering a few clarifications or additional details, but little more. Other journalists, however, sense a growing partnership between news organizations and citizens in which individuals originate a significant portion of the news. These partnerships seem especially likely in regard to local issues and offer an opportunity for the news media to present expanded coverage within the constraints of their limited professional resources. Again, this will increase the voice of the public in the news agenda and its corollary influence on public officials.

Ultimately, these partnerships between the public and the news media may link up with a variety of efforts to build direct partnerships between citizens and their government. These efforts range from the creation of broad-based forums that seek to foster ongoing conversations for the evolution of public policy to the very focused and highly defined goals of deliberative polling, in which a representative sample of the public come together to learn, deliberate, and then express their opinions about a particular issue, such as the mix of sources of energy for generating electricity. Although these efforts generally do not include the news media as explicit partners, we know from our examination of media effects that the media can have a significant indirect effect on these conversations.

Curtain call

Central in the formation of public opinion are the stages of the communication process that have been discussed in the previous chapters: stages that define a hierarchy of media effects extending from exposure to manifest observable behavior. Although the contemporary media landscape is now changing and expanding at a rapid rate, the principles summarized by this hierarchy of effects continue to be relevant and basic to the political communication process. News media influence is fundamentally a story about process. Although new channels of communication may embellish and alter to some degree the salience of some aspects of these processes of influence, they will continue to be the central story of political communication and the formation of public opinion.

Notes

Introduction: What Is Public Opinion?

1 Jürgen Habermas, *The Theory of Communicative Action*, trans. Thomas McCarthy (Boston, Mass.: Beacon Press, 1984).
2 John Dewey, *The Public and Its Problems* (Athens, Ohio: Swallow, 1927).
3 Roger Fidler, *MediaMorphosis: Understanding New Media* (Thousand Oaks, Calif.: Pine Forge Press, 1997).
4 Paul Lazarsfeld, Bernard Berelson, and Hazel Gaudet, *The People's Choice* (New York: Columbia University Press, 1944).
5 James Bryce, *The American Commonwealth* (New York: Macmillan, 1910).
6 Gabriel Tarde, *L'opinion et la foule* (Paris: F. Alcan, 1901).

Chapter 1: A Changing Communication Environment

1 Markus Prior, *Post-Broadcast Democracy: How Media Choice Increases Inequality in Political Involvement and Polarizes Elections* (New York: Cambridge University Press, 2007).
2 Geoffrey Baym, "*The Daily Show*: discursive integration and the reinvention of political journalism," *Political Communication* 22 (2005), pp. 259–76.
3 Roderick Hart and E. Johanna Hartelius, "The political sins of Jon Stewart," *Critical Studies in Media Communication* 24 (2007), pp. 263–72.
4 Wolfram Peiser, "Cohort replacement and the downward trend in newspaper readership," *Newspaper Research Journal* 21 (2000), pp. 11–22.
5 Carl Sessions Stepp, "Why do people read newspapers?" *American Journalism Review* 25 (2003/2004), pp. 64–69.
6 Mike Conway, Maria Elizabeth Grabe, and Kevin Grieves, "Villains, victims, and the virtuous in Bill O'Reilly's 'No-Spin Zone': Revisiting world war propaganda techniques," *Journalism Studies* 8 (2007), pp. 197–223.
7 Josh Getlin, "Fox News' patriotic fervor sets it apart in ratings race," *The Los Angeles Times*, April 11, 2003.

8 Eric Deggans, "In TV war news, the hits and misses," *St. Petersburg Times*, April 14, 2003.

9 Chris Bedouin, Michael Antecol, and Esther Thorson, "Fox News: Fostering or fomenting support for the war in Iraq," paper presented to the Association for Education in Journalism and Mass Communication, Kansas City, August, 2003.

10 Jonathan Morris, "Slanted objectivity? Perceived media bias, cable news exposure and political attitudes," *Social Science Quarterly* 88 (2007), pp. 707–28.

11 Jonathan Morris, "The Fox News factor," *Harvard International Journal of Press/Politics* 10 (2005), pp. 56–79.

12 David Barker, *Rushed to Judgment: Talk Radio, Persuasion, and American Political Behavior* (New York: Columbia University Press, 2002).

13 John Merrill and Ralph Lowenstein, *Media, Messages and Men: New Perspectives in Communication* (New York: David McKay, 1971).

14 Wayne Wanta, Stephanie Craft, and M. Geana, "News media choices and the polarization of attitudes," paper presented to the International Communication Association, New York City, 2005.

15 Michiko Kakutani, "Is Jon Stewart the most trusted man in America?," Nytimes.com, http://www.nytimes.com/2008/08/17/arts/television/17kaku.html?_r=1&pagewanted=print&oref=slogin (accessed September 4, 2008).

16 Robert Lance Holbert, "A typology for the study of entertainment television and politics," *American Behavioral Scientist* 49 (2005), pp. 436–53.

17 Baym, *"The Daily Show."*

18 Hart and Hartelius, "The political sins."

19 Robert Lance Holbert, Jennifer Lambe, Anthony Dudo, and Kristen Carlton, "Primacy effects of *The Daily Show* and national TV news viewing: young viewers, political gratifications, and internal political self-efficacy," *Journal of Broadcasting & Electronic Media* 51 (2007), pp. 20–38.

20 Dannagal Young and Russell Tisinger, "Dispelling late-night myths: news consumption among late-night comedy viewers and the predictors of exposure to various late-night shows," *Harvard International Journal of Press/Politics* 11 (2006), pp. 113–34.

21 Julia Fox, Glory Koloen, and Volkan Sahin, "No joke: a comparison of substance in *The Daily Show with Jon Stewart* and broadcast network television coverage of the 2004 presidential election campaign," *Journal of Broadcasting & Electronic Media* 51 (2007), pp. 213–27.

22 Patricia Moy and Michael Pfau, *With Malice Toward All? The Media and Public Confidence in Democratic Institutions* (Westport, Conn.: Praeger, 2000).

23 Holbert et al., "Primacy effects of *The Daily Show*."

24 Conway et al., "Villains, victims, and the virtuous."

25 Mark Leibovich, "Media bashing 101," Nytimes.com, http://www.nytimes.

com/2008/09/07/weekinreview/07leibovich.html?_r=1&ref=politics&oref=s login (accessed September 6, 2008).

26 Marion Just, Ann Crigler, Dean Alger, Timothy Cook, Montague Kern, and Darrell West, *Crosstalk: Citizens, Candidates, and the Media in a Presidential Campaign* (Chicago: University of Chicago Press, 1996).

27 Matthew Baum, *Soft News Goes to War* (Princeton, N.J.: Princeton University Press, 2003).

28 Young and Tisinger, "Dispelling late-night myths."

29 See Robert Lance Holbert and Glenn Hansen, "Stepping beyond message specificity in the study of emotion as mediator and inter-emotion associations across attitude objects: *Fahrenheit 9/11*, anger, and debate superiority," *Media Psychology* 11 (2008), pp. 98–118, for full listing of studies.

30 Diana Mutz, "The future of political communication research: Reflections on the occasion of Steve Chaffee's retirement from Stanford University," *Political Communication* 18 (2001), pp. 231–36.

Chapter 2: Reporting the News

1 Kurt Lewin, "Frontiers in group dynamics: concept methods and reality in social equilibria and social change," *Human Relations* 1, 1 (1947), pp. 5–41.

2 David Manning White, "The 'Gate keeper': a case study in the selection of news, *Journalism Quarterly* 27, 3 (1950), pp. 383–90.

3 David H. Weaver and G. Cleveland Wilhoit, *The American Journalist: A Portrait of U.S. Newspeople and Their Work* (Bloomington: Indiana University Press, 1986); David H. Weaver and G. Cleveland Wilhoit, *The American Journalist in the 1990s: U.S. News People at the End of an Era* (Mahwah, N.J.: Lawrence Erlbaum, 1996); David H. Weaver, Randal Beam, Bonnie Brownlee, Paul S. Voakes, and G. Cleveland Wilhoit, *The American Journalist in the 21st Century: U.S. News People at the Dawn of a New Millennium* (Mahwah, N.J.: Lawrence Erlbaum, 2007).

4 Dan Berkowitz, "Assessing forces in the selection of local television news," *Journal of Broadcasting & Electronic Media*, 34 (1991), pp. 55–68.

5 Pamela J. Shoemaker, Martin Eichholz, Eunyi Kim and Brenda Wrigley, "Individual and routine forces in gatekeeping," *Journalism & Mass Communication Quarterly* 78 (2001), pp. 233–47.

6 Gaye Tuchman, *Making News: A Study in the Construction of Reality* (New York: The Free Press, 1978).

7 Warren Breed, "Social control in the newsroom: a functional analysis," *Social Forces* 33, 4 (1955), pp. 326–35.

8 James T. Hamilton, *All the News That's Fit to Sell: How the Market Transforms Information into News* (Princeton, N.J.: Princeton University Press, 2004).

9 H. Shik Kim, "Gatekeeping international news: an attitudinal profile of U.S.

television journalists," *Journal of Broadcasting & Electronic Media* 46 (2002), pp. 431–52.

10 Todd Gitlin, *The Whole World Is Watching* (Berkeley: University of California Press, 1980).

11 Wayne Wanta, Mary Ann Stephenson, Judy VanSlyke Turk, and Maxwell McCombs, "How President's State of Union talk influenced news media agendas," *Journalism Quarterly* 66, 3 (1989), pp. 537–41.

12 James N. Druckman and Michael Parkin, "The impact of media bias: how editorial slant affects voters," *The Journal of Politics* 67 (2005), pp. 1030–49.

13 Jim A. Kuypers, *Press Bias and Politics: How the Media Frame Controversial Issues* (New York: Praeger, 2002); S. Robert Lichter, Stanley Rothman, and Linda S. Lichter, *The Media Elite: America's New Power Brokers* (Bethesda, Md.: Adler and Adler, 1986); Daniel Okrent, "The Public Editor: is *The New York Times* a liberal newspaper?," *The New York Times*, July 25, 2004, p. 42.

14 Kuypers, *Press Bias And Politics*.

15 Stephen J. Farnsworth and S. Robert Lichter, "The mediated congress: coverage of Capitol Hill in the *The New York Times* and *The Washington Post*," *Harvard International Journal of Press/Politics* 10 (2005), pp. 97–107.

16 Adam Schiffer, "Assessing partisan bias in political news: the case(s) of local Senate election coverage," *Political Communication* 23 (2006), pp. 23–39.

17 Eric Alterman, *What Liberal Media? The Truth about Bias and the News* (New York: Basic Books, 2003).

18 Geoffrey Numberg, "Media: label whores," *The American Prospect*, May 5, 2002.

19 Weaver and Wilhoit, *The American Journalist in the 1990s*.

20 David Niven, "Bias in the news: partisanship and negativity in media coverage of presidents George Bush and Bill Clinton," *The Harvard International Journal of Press/Politics* 6 (2001), pp. 31–46.

21 Dave D'Alessio and Mike Allen, "Media bias in presidential elections: a meta-analysis," *Journal of Communication* 50 (2000), pp. 133–56.

22 Mark D. Watts, David Domke, Dhavan V. Shah, and David P. Fan, "Elite cues and media bias in presidential campaigns: explaining public perceptions of a liberal press," *Communication Research* 26 (1999), pp. 144–75.

23 Kathleen M. Schmitt, Albert C. Gunther, and Janice L. Liebhart, "Why partisans see mass media as biased," *Communication Research* 31 (2004), pp. 623–41.

24 Jane B. Singer, "The political J-Blogger: normalizing a new media form to fit old norms and practices," paper presented to the Association for Education in Journalism and Mass Communication, New Orleans, 2004.

25 Bruce A. Williams and Michael X. Deli Carpini, "Unchained reaction: the

collapse of media gatekeeping and the Clinton-Lewinsky scandal," *Journalism* 1 (2000), pp. 61–85.

26 Jay Rosen, "Questions and answers about public journalism," *Journalism Studies* 1 (2000), pp. 679–83.

27 Arthur Charity, *Doing Public Journalism* (New York: Guilford Press, 1995).

28 Frank Denton and Esther Thorson, "Effects of a multimedia public journalism project on political knowledge and attitudes," in *Assessing Public Journalism*, ed. Edmund B. Lambeth, Phillip E. Meyer, and Esther Thorson (Columbia: University of Missouri Press, 1998).

29 Esther Thorson, Ekaterina Ognianova, James Coyle, and Edmund B. Lambeth, "Audience impact of a multimedia civic journalism project in a small midwestern community," in *Assessing Public Journalism*, ed. Edmund B. Lambeth, Phillip E. Meyer, and Esther Thorson.

30 Tanni Haas, "Public journalism project falls short of stated goals," *Newspaper Research Journal* 22 (2001), pp. 58–70; Edwin Diamond, "Civic journalism: An experiment that didn't work," *Columbia Journalism Review* 36 (1997), pp. 11–12.

Chapter 3: Trust in the News

1 James McCroskey and Jason Neven, "Goodwill: A reexamination of the construct and its measurement," *Communication Monographs* 66 (1999), pp. 90–103.

2 Matt Carlson, "War journalism and the 'KIA journalist': the cases of David Bloom and Michael Kelly," *Critical Studies in Media Communication* 23 (2006), pp. 91–111.

3 Shyam Sundar, "Exploring receivers' criteria for perception of print and online news," *Journalism & Mass Communication Quarterly* 76 (1999), pp. 373–86; Erik Bucy, "Media credibility reconsidered: synergy effects between on-air and online news. *Journalism & Mass Communication Quarterly* 80 (2003), pp. 247–64.

4 Cecilie Gaziano and Kristin McGrath, "Measuring the concept of credibility," *Journalism Quarterly* 63 (1986), pp. 451–62.

5 Matthias Kohring and Jörg Matthes, "Trust in news media: development and validation of a multidimensional scale," *Communication Research* 34 (2007), pp. 231–52.

6 Wolfgang Schweiger, "Media credibility—experience or image? A survey on the credibility of the World Wide Web in Germany in comparison to other media," *European Journal of Communication* 15 (2000), pp. 37–59.

7 Michael Schudson, "The public journalism movement and its problems," in *The Politics of News: The News of Politics*, ed. Doris Graber, Denis McQuail, and Pippa Norris (Washington, D.C.: Congressional Quarterly Press, 1998), pp. 132–49.

8 Markus Prior, *Post-Broadcast Democracy: How Media Choice Increases Inequality in Political Involvement and Polarizes Elections* (New York: Cambridge University Press, 2007).

9 Richard Kaplan, "The news about new institutionalism: journalism's ethic of objectivity and its political origins," *Political Communication* 23 (2006), pp. 173–85, p. 177.

10 Ibid., p. 179.

11 Thomas Patterson, "Political roles of the journalist", in *The Politics of News: The News of Politics*, ed. Doris Graber, Denis McQuail and Pippa Norris (Washington, D.C.: Congressional Quarterly Press, 1998), pp. 17–32.

12 Schudson, "The public journalism movement and its problems," p. 136.

13 Walter Lippmann, "Two revolutions in the American press," in *The Essential Lippmann: A Political Philosophy for Liberal Democracy*, ed. Clinton Rossiter and James Lance (Cambridge, Mass.: Harvard University Press, 1982), pp. 402–6.

14 Jay Rosen, *Getting the Connections Right* (New York: Twentieth Century Fund, 1996); Kaplan, "The news about new institutionalism," p. 181; James Tankard, Jr., "Reporting and scientific method," in *Handbook of Reporting Methods*, ed. Maxwell McCombs, Donald Shaw, and David Grey (Boston: Houghton Mifflin, 1976), pp. 42–77.

15 Christopher Beaudoin and Esther Thorson, "A marketplace theory of media use," *Mass Communication & Society* 5 (2002), pp. 241–62.

16 Thomas Johnson and Shahira Fahmy, "The CNN of the Arab world or shill for terrorists? How support for press freedom and political ideology predict credibility of Al-Jazeera among its audience," paper presented to the International Communication Association, New York, 2005.

17 Ali Jamal and Srinivas Melkote, "Viewing and avoidance of the Al-Jazeera satellite television channel in Kuwait: a uses and gratifications perspective," *Asian Journal of Communication* 18 (2008), pp. 1–15.

18 Wayne Wanta and Yu-Wei Hu, "The effects of credibility, reliance, and exposure on media agenda-setting: A path analysis model," *Journalism Quarterly* 71 (1994), pp. 90–98.

19 Ronald Mulder, "Media credibility: A uses-gratifications approach," *Journalism Quarterly* 57 (1980), pp. 474–77.

20 Spiro Kiousis, "Public trust or mistrust? Perceptions of media credibility in the information age," *Mass Communication & Society* 4 (2001), pp. 381–403; Wanta and Hu, "The effects of credibility."

21 Andrew Flanagin and Miriam Metzger, "Perceptions of internet information credibility," *Journalism & Mass Communication Quarterly* 77 (2000), pp. 515–40.

22 Kiousis, "Public trust or mistrust?"; Schweiger, "Media credibility—experience or image?"

23 Debra Melican and Travis Dixon, "News on the net: Credibility, selective

exposure, and racial prejudice," *Communication Research* 35 (2008), pp. 151–68.

24 Bucy, "Media credibility reconsidered."

25 Sundar, "Exploring receivers' criteria."

26 Rasha Abdulla, Bruce Garrison, Michael Salwen, Paul Driscoll, and Denise Casey, "Online news credibility," in *Online News and the Public*, ed. Michael Salwen, Bruce Garrison, and Paul Driscoll (Mahwah, N.J.: Lawrence Erlbaum Associates, 2005), pp. 147–64.

27 Eric Alterman, "Out of print: The death and life of the American newspaper," *The New Yorker*, March 31, 2008, pp. 48–59.

28 Ibid., p. 51.

29 McCroskey and Neven, "Goodwill: a reexamination," p. 90.

30 Ibid., p. 92.

31 Ibid., p. 90.

32 Ibid., p. 92.

33 James Fallows, "The age of Murdoch," theatlantic.com, http://www.the atlantic.com/doc/200309/fallows (accessed April 1, 2008).

34 Sylvia Chan-Olmsted, "Branding television news in a multichannel environment: An exploratory study of network news brand personality," *International Journal of Media Management* 4 (2007), pp. 135–50.

35 Mike Conway, Maria Elizabeth Grabe, and Kevin Grieves, "Villains, victims, and the virtuous in Bill O'Reilly's "No-Spin Zone": revisiting world war propaganda techniques," *Journalism Studies* 8 (2007), pp. 197–223.

36 Michael Slater, "Reinforcing spirals: the mutual influence of media selectivity and media effects and their impact on individual behavior and social identity," *Communication Theory* 17 (2007), pp. 281–303.

37 Stephen Bennett, "Predicting Americans' exposure to political talk radio in 1996, 1998, and 2000," *Harvard International Journal of Press/Politics* 7 (2002), pp. 9–22.

38 Geoffrey Baym, "*The Daily Show*: Discursive integration and the reinvention of political journalism," *Political Communication* 22 (2005), p. 262.

39 Charles A. Knight, *The Literature of Satire* (Cambridge, U.K.: Cambridge University Press, 2004), p. 4.

40 Leonard Feinberg, *Introduction to Satire* (Ames: The Iowa State University Press, 1967).

41 Robert Lance Holbert, Jennifer Lambe, Anthony Dudo, and Kristen Carlton, "Primacy effects of *The Daily Show* and national TV news viewing: young viewers, political gratifications, and internal political self-efficacy," *Journal of Broadcasting & Electronic Media* 51 (2007), pp. 20–38.

Chapter 4: The Audiences for News

1 James Webster, "The audience," *Journal of Broadcasting & Electronic Media* 42 (1998), pp. 190–207.

2 James Webster and Patricia Phalen, *The Mass Audience: Rediscovering the Dominant Model* (Mahwah, N.J.: Lawrence Erlbaum Associates, 1997), p. 1 (italics in original).

3 Steven Chaffee and Joan Schleuder, "Measurement and effects of attention to media news," *Human Communication Research* 13 (1986), pp. 76–107.

4 Ibid., p. 104. See also William P. Eveland, Jr., Myiah J. Hutchens, and Fei Shen, "Exposure, attention, or 'use' of news? Assessing aspects of the reliability and validity of a central concept in political communication research," *Communication Methods and Measures* 3 (2009), pp. 223–44.

5 Markus Prior, "The immensely inflated news audience: assessing bias in self-reported news exposure," *Public Opinion Quarterly* 73 (2009), pp. 130–43.

6 Anca Romantan, Robert Hornick, Vincent Price, Joseph Cappella, and K. Viswanath, "A comparative analysis of the performance of alternative measures of exposure," *Communication Methods and Measures* 1, 2 (2008), pp. 80–99.

7 Chul-Joo Lee, Robert Hornick, and Michael Hennessey, "The reliability and stability of general media exposure measures," *Communication Methods and Measures* 1, 2 (2008), pp. 6–22.

8 Dannagal Young and Russell Tisinger, "Dispelling late-night myths: news consumption among late-night comedy viewers and the predictors of exposure to various late-night shows," *Harvard International Journal of Press/Politics* 11 (2006), pp. 113–34.

9 Douglas Ahlers, "News consumption and the new electronic media," *Harvard International Journal of Press/Politics* 11 (2006), pp. 29–52.

10 Matthew Baum, *Soft News Goes to War* (Princeton, N.J.: Princeton University Press, 2003).

11 Lauren Feldman and Dannagal Young, "Late-night comedy as a gateway to traditional news: an analysis of time trends in news attention among late-night comedy viewers during the 2004 presidential primaries," *Political Communication* 25 (2008), pp. 401–22.

12 Paul Lazarsfeld, Barnard Berelson, and Hazel Gaudet, *The People's Choice* (New York: Columbia University Press, 1944), p. 122.

13 Jack McLeod, Dietram Scheufele, and Patricia Moy, "Community, communication, and participation: the role of mass media and interpersonal discussion in local political participation," *Political Communication* 16 (1999), pp. 315–36.

14 Dhavan Shah and Dietram Scheufele, "Explicating opinion leadership:

nonpolitical dispositions, information consumption, and civic participation," *Political Communication* 23 (2006), pp. 1–22.

15 R. Lance Holbert, "Debate viewing as mediator and partisan reinforcement in the relationship between news use and vote choice," *Journal of Communication* 55 (2005), pp. 85–102.

16 R. Lance Holbert and William Benoit, "A theory of political campaign media connectedness," *Communication Monographs* 76 (2009), pp. 303–32.

17 John Zaller, *The Nature and Origins of Mass Opinion* (New York: Cambridge University Press, 1992).

18 Markus Prior, *Post-Broadcast Democracy: How Media Choice Increases Inequality in Political Involvement and Polarizes Elections* (New York: Cambridge University Press, 2007).

Chapter 5: Focusing Public Attention

1 See for example Carl I. Hovland, O. J. Harvey, and Muzafer Sherif, "Assimilation and contrast effects in reactions to communication and attitude change," *Journal of Abnormal and Social Psychology* 55 (1957), pp. 244–252; Muzafer Sherif and Carl I. Hovland, *Social Judgment: Assimilation and Contrast Effects in Communication and Attitude Change* (New Haven: Yale University Press, 1961); and Paul Lazarsfeld, Bernard Berelson, and Hazel Gaudet, *The People's Choice* (New York: Columbia University Press, 1944).

2 Joseph T. Klapper, *The Effects of Mass Communication* (Glencoe, Ill.: Free Press, 1960).

3 Bernard C. Cohen, *The Press and Foreign Policy* (Princeton, N.J.: Princeton University Press, 1963), p. 20 (emphasis added).

4 Maxwell McCombs and Donald Shaw, "The agenda-setting function of mass media," *Public Opinion Quarterly* 36 (1972), pp. 176–87.

5 Donald Lewis Shaw and Maxwell E. McCombs, *The Emergence of American Political Issues* (St. Paul, Minn.: West, 1977).

6 Shanto Iyengar and Donald R Kinder, *News that Matters* (Chicago: University of Chicago Press, 1987); Shanto Iyengar, Mark D. Peters, and Donald Kinder, "Experimental demonstrations of the 'not-so-minimal' consequences of television news programs," *American Political Science Review* 76 (1982), pp. 848–58; Shanto Iyengar, Mark D. Peters, Donald Kinder, and Jon A. Krosnick, "The evening news and presidential evaluations," *Journal of Personality and Social Psychology* 46 (1984), pp. 778–87.

7 Shanto Iyengar, "How citizens think about national issues: a matter of responsibility." *American Journal of Political Science* 33 (1989), pp. 879–99; Iyengar et al., "The evening news and presidential evaluations,"

8 G. Ray Funkhouser, "Trends in media coverage of the issues of the sixties," *Journalism Quarterly* 50 (1973), pp. 533–38.

9 James P. Winter and Chaim H. Eyal, "Agenda-setting for the civil rights issue," *Public Opinion Quarterly* 45 (1981), pp. 376–83.
10 Deborah J. Blood and Peter C. B. Phillips, "Economic headline news on the agenda: new approaches to understanding cause and effects," in *Communication and Democracy: Exploring the Intellectual Frontiers in Agenda-Setting Theory*, ed. Maxwell McCombs, Donald Shaw, and David Weaver (Mahwah, N.J.: Lawrence Erlbaum, 1997), pp. 97–113.
11 Michael B. Mackuen and Steven Lane Coombs, *More than News: Media Power in Public Affairs* (Beverly Hills, Calif.: Sage, 1981).
12 Stuart N. Soroka, "Media, public opinion, and foreign policy," *Harvard International Journal of Press/Politics* 8 (2003), pp. 27–48.
13 Klaus Schoenbach, "Agenda-setting effects of print and television in West Germany," in *Agenda-Setting: Readings on Media, Public Opinion and Policymaking*, ed. Maxwell McCombs (Hillsdale, N.J.: Lawrence Erlbaum, 1991), pp. 127–29.
14 Toshio Takeshita, "Current critical problems in agenda-setting research," *International Journal of Public Opinion Research* 18 (2006), pp. 275–96.
15 Federico Rey Lennon, "Argentina: 1997 elecciones: los diarios nacionales y la campana electoral [The 1997 Argentina election: the national dailies and the electoral campaign]," Report by The Freedom Forum and Austral University, 1998.
16 Salma Ghanem and Wayne Wanta, "Agenda setting and Spanish cable news," *Journal of Broadcast & Electronic Media* 45 (2001), pp. 277–89.
17 Harold Zucker, "The variable nature of news media influence," in *Communication Yearbook 2*, ed. Brent D. Ruben (New Brunswick , N.J.: Transaction Books, 1978), pp. 225–45.
18 David H. Weaver, "Political issues and voter need for orientation', in *The Emergence of American Political Issues: The Agenda Setting Function of the Press*, ed. Maxwell McCombs and Donald Shaw (St. Paul, Minn.: West Publishers, 1977), pp. 107–19.
19 Joanne Miller, "Examining the mediators of agenda setting: a new experimental paradigm reveals the role of emotions," *Political Psychology* 28 (2007), pp. 689–717.
20 Renita Coleman and Maxwell McCombs, "The young and agenda-less: exploring age-related differences in agenda setting on the youngest generation, Baby Boomers, and the Civic Generation," *Journalism & Mass Communication Quarterly* 84 (2007), pp. 495–508.
21 Donald Shaw and Shannon E. Martin, "The function of mass media agenda setting," *Journalism Quarterly* 69 (1992), pp. 902–20.
22 Ying Du, "The role of mass media in achieving social consensus: an agenda-melding study," paper presented to the International Communication Association, San Francisco, 2007.
23 David Weaver, Doris Graber, Maxwell McCombs, and Chaim Eyal, *Media*

Agenda-Setting in a Presidential Election: Issues, Images, and Interests (New York: Praeger, 1981).

24 Gyotae Ku, Lynda Lee Kaid, and Michael Pfau, "The impact of web site campaigning on traditional news media and public information processing," *Journalism & Mass Communication Quarterly* 80 (2003), pp. 528–47.

25 Maxwell E. McCombs, *Setting the Agenda: The Mass Media and Public Opinion* (Cambridge, U.K.: Polity, 2004), p. 69.

26 Charles Fombrun and Mark Shanley, "What's in a name? Reputation building and corporate strategy," *Academy of Management Journal* 33 (1990), pp. 233–58.

27 Wayne Wanta, Guy Golan, and Cheolhan Lee, "Agenda setting and international news: media influence on public perceptions of foreign nations," *Journalism & Mass Communication Quarterly* 81 (2004), pp. 364–77.

28 Maxwell E. McCombs and Salma I. Ghanem, "The convergence of agenda setting and framing," in *Framing Public Life: Perspectives on Media and Our Understanding of the World,* ed. Stephen D. Reese, Oscar H. Gandy, Jr., and August E. Grant (Mahwah, N.J.: Lawrence Erlbaum, 2001), pp. 67–82, p. 68.

29 Hsiang Iris Chyi and Maxwell McCombs, "Media salience and the process of framing: coverage of the Columbine school shootings," *Journalism & Mass Communication Quarterly* 81 (2004), pp. 22–35, p. 24.

30 Guy Golan and Wayne Wanta, "Second-level agenda setting in the New Hampshire primary: a comparison of coverage in three newspapers and public perceptions of candidates," *Journalism & Mass Communication Quarterly,* 78 (2001), pp. 247–59.

31 Maxwell McCombs, Esteban Lopez-Escobar, and Juan Pablo Llamas, "Setting the agenda of attributes in the 1996 Spanish general election," *Journal of Communication* 50, 2 (2000), pp. 77–92.

32 Marc Benton and P. Jean Frazier, "The agenda-setting function of the mass media at three levels of information holding," *Communication Research* 3 (1976), pp. 261–74.

33 Stephanie Craft and Wayne Wanta, "U.S. public concerns in the aftermath of 9–11: a test of second-level agenda-setting," *International Journal of Public Opinion Research* 16 (2004), pp. 456–62.

34 Spiro Kiousis, "Compelling argument and attitude strength: exploring the impact of second-level agenda-setting on public opinion of presidential candidate images," *Harvard International Journal of Press/Politics* 10 (2005), pp. 3–27.

Chapter 6: Learning from the News

1 Doris Graber, *Processing the News: How People Tame the Information Tide* (Lanham, Md.: University Press of America, 1988).

2 Raymond S. Nickerson, "Short-term memory for complex meaningful visual

configurations: a demonstration of capacity," *Canadian Journal of Psychology* 19 (1965), pp. 155–60.

3 Michael X. Delli Carpini and Scott Keeter, *What Americans Know About Politics and Why It Matters* (New Haven, Conn.: Yale University Press, 1996).

4 Robert D. McClure and Thomas E. Patterson, "Television news and political advertising: the impact of exposure on voter beliefs," *Communication Research* 1 (1974), pp. 3–31; Wojciech Cwalina and Andrzej Falkowski, "Political communication and advertising in Poland," in *The Sage Handbook of Political Advertising*, ed. Lynda Lee Kaid and Christina Holtz-Bacha (Newbury Park, Calif.: Sage, 2000), pp. 325–42.

5 Stephen Ansolabehere and Shanto Iyengar, *Going Negative: How Political Advertisements Shrink and Polarize the Electorate* (New York: Free Press, 1995).

6 Phillip J. Tichenor, George A. Donohue, and Clarice N. Olien, "Mass media and the differential growth in knowledge," *Public Opinion Quarterly* 34 (1970), pp. 158–70.

7 Kasisomayajula Viswanath and John R. Finnegan, "The knowledge gap hypothesis: twenty-five years later," *Communication Yearbook* 19 (1996), pp. 187–227.

8 Richard E. Petty and John T. Cacioppo, "Issue involvement can increase or decrease persuasion by enhancing message-relevant cognitive responses," *Journal of Personality and Social Psychology* 37 (1979), pp. 1915–26.

9 Anthony Downs, *An Economic Theory of Democracy* (New York: Harper, 1957).

10 Michael Schudson, *The Good Citizen: A History of American Civic Life* (New York: Free Press, 1998).

11 Samuel L. Popkin, *The Reasoning Voter* (Chicago: University of Chicago Press, 1994).

12 William P. Eveland, "The cognitive mediation model of learning from the news," *Communication Research* 28, 5 (2001), pp. 571–601; and "News information processing as mediator of the relationship between motivations and political knowledge," *Journalism & Mass Communication Quarterly* 79 (2002), pp. 26–40.

13 Eliot R. Smith, "Mental representation and memory," in *The Handbook of Social Psychology, 4th ed.*, ed. Daniel T. Gilbert, Susan T. Fiske, and Gardner Lindzey (New York: Oxford University Press, 1988), pp. 391–445.

Chapter 7: Forming Opinions

1 Paul Lazarsfeld, Bernard Berelson, and Hazel Gaudet, *The People's Choice* (New York: Columbia University Press, 1948).

2 Ibid., p. 87 (emphasis added).

3 Joseph T. Klapper, *The Effects of Mass Communication*, (Glencoe, Ill.: Free Press, 1960).

4 See for example, Lee B. Becker, Maxwell E. McCombs, and Jack M. McLeod, "The development of political cognitions," in *Political Communication: Issues and Strategies for Research*, ed. Steven H. Chaffee (Beverly Hills, Calif.: Sage, 1975), pp. 121–64.

5 Larry M. Bartels, "Messages received: the political impact of media exposure," *American Political Science Review* 87 (1993), pp. 267–85.

6 Kamal Abouchedid and Ramsi Nasser, "Info-bias mechanism and American college students' attitudes towards Arabs," *International Studies Perspectives* 7 (2006), pp. 204–12.

7 Benjamin I. Page and Robert Y. Shapiro, *The Rational Public: Fifty Years of Trends in Americans' Policy Preferences* (Chicago: University of Chicago Press, 1992).

8 John Zaller, *The Nature and Origins of Mass Opinion* (New York: Cambridge University Press, 1992).

9 Ibid., p. 37 (emphasis added).

10 Gangheong H. Lee and Joseph N. Cappella, "The effects of political talk radio on political attitude formation: exposure versus knowledge," *Political Communication* 18 (2001), pp. 369–94.

11 Spiro Kiousis, Michael McDevitt, and Xu Wu, "The genesis of civic awareness: agenda setting in political socialization," *Journal of Communication* 55 (2005), pp. 756–74.

12 G. M. Garramone, "TV news and adolescent political socialization," *Communication Yearbook* 7 (1983), pp. 651–67.

13 David Weaver, "Issue salience and public opinion: are there consequences of agenda-setting?" *International Journal of Public Opinion Research* 3 (1991), pp. 53–68.

14 Sei-Hill Kim, Dietram A. Scheufele and James Shanahan, "Who cares about the issues? Issue voting and the role of news media during the 2000 U.S. Presidential Election," *Journal of Communication* 55 (2005), pp. 103–21.

15 See, for example, Shanto Iyengar, Mark D. Peters, and Donald Kinder, "Experimental demonstrations of the 'not-so-minimal' consequences of television news programs," *American Political Science Review* 76 (1982), pp. 848–58; Shanto Iyengar, Mark D. Peters, Donald Kinder, and Jon A. Krosnick, "The evening news and presidential evaluations," *Journal of Personality and Social Psychology* 46 (1984), pp. 778–87; and Roy Behr and Shanto Iyengar, "Television news, real world cues, and changes in the public agenda," *Public Opinion Quarterly* 49 (1985), pp. 38–57.

16 Tamir Sheafer and Gabriel Weimann, "Agenda building, agenda setting, priming, individual voting intentions, and the aggregate results: an analysis of four Israeli elections," *Journal of Communication* 20 (2005), pp. 347–65.

17 Thomas Nelson, Zoe M. Oxley, and Rosalee A. Clawson, "Towards a

psychology of framing effects," *Political Behavior* 19 (1997), pp. 221–46, 236 (emphasis in original).

18 Daniel Romer, Kathleen Hall Jamieson, and Sean Aday, "Television news and the cultivation of fear of crime," *Journal of Communication* 53 (2003), pp. 88–104.

19 Larry Sabato, "Open season: how the news media cover presidential campaigns in the age of attack journalism," in *Media Power in Politics,* ed. Doris A. Graber (Washington, D.C.: Congressional Quarterly Press, 1994), pp. 161–71, p. 168.

20 Joseph N. Cappella and Kathleen Hall Jamieson, *Spiral of Cynicism: The Press and the Public Good* (New York: Oxford University Press, 1997).

21 Robert D. Putnam, "Tuning in, tuning out: the strange disappearance of social capital in America," *PS: Political Science and Politics* 28 (1995), pp. 664–83.

22 John Brehm and Wendy Rahn, "Individual-level evidence for the causes and consequences of social capital," *American Journal of Political Science* 41 (1997), pp. 999–1023.

23 Kenneth Newton, "Mass media effects: mobilization or media malaise?," *British Journal of Political Science* 29 (1999), pp. 577–99.

24 Christina Holtz-Bacha, "Videomalaise revisited: media exposure and political alienation in West Germany," *European Journal of Communication* 5 (1990), pp. 73–85; Shelley Boulianne, "Does Internet use affect engagement? A meta-analysis of research," *Political Communication* 26, 2 (2009) pp. 193–211.

25 See, for example, Hirotada Hirose, Naoko Nakaune, Tomoichi Ishizuka, Shoji Tsuchida and Yasue Takanashi, "A study on the role of AIDS mass communication: how do the mass media affect HIV testing behavior?" *Japanese Psychological Research* 40 (1998), pp. 246–55.

Chapter 8: The Tone of the News

1 Spiro Kiousis, "Explicating media salience: a factor analysis of *New York Times* issue coverage during the 2000 presidential election," *Journal of Communication* 54 (2004), pp. 71–87.

2 Dixie Evatt and Salma Ghanem, "Building a scale to measure salience," paper presented to the World Association for Public Opinion Research, Rome, Italy, 2001.

3 Joanne Miller, "Examining the mediators of agenda setting: a new experimental paradigm reveals the role of emotions," *Political Psychology* 28 (2007), pp. 689–717.

4 Maxwell McCombs, Esteban Lopez-Escobar, and Juan Pablo Llamas, "Setting the agenda of attributes in the 1996 Spanish general election," *Journal of Communication* 50, 2 (2000), pp. 77–92.

5 Maxwell McCombs, Juan Pablo Llamas, Esteban Lopez-Escobar, and Federico Rey, "Candidate images in Spanish elections: second-level agenda setting effects," *Journalism & Mass Communication Quarterly* 74 (1997), pp. 703–17.

6 Kihan Kim and Maxwell McCombs, "News story descriptions and the public's opinions of political candidates," *Journalism & Mass Communication Quarterly* 84 (2007), pp. 299–314.

7 Ingrid Bachmann, "Affective behavior effects in electoral politics: an exploratory analysis of attribute agenda-setting effects via emotional traits in news stories," paper presented to the Seminar on Agenda-Setting Theory, University of Texas at Austin, 2009.

8 Meital Balmas and Tamir Sheafer, "Candidate image in election campaigns: attribute agenda-setting, affective priming and voting intentions," paper presented to the International Communication Association, Chicago, 2009.

9 Young Jun Son and David Weaver, "Another look at what moves public opinion: media agenda setting and polls in the 2000 U.S. election," *International Journal of Public Opinion Research* 18 (2006), pp. 174–97.

10 Daron Shaw, "The impact of news media favorability and candidate events in presidential campaigns," *Political Communication* 16 (1999), pp. 183–202.

11 Jeffrey Cohen, *The Presidency in the Era of 24-hour News* (Princeton, N.J.: Princeton University Press, 2008).

12 Richard Brody, *Assessing Presidential Character: The Media, Elite Opinion, and Public Support* (Stanford, Calif.: Stanford University Press, 1991).

13 Hans Mathias Kepplinger, Wolfgang Donsbach, Hans Bernd Brosius, and Joachim Friedrich Staab, "Media tone and public opinion: a longitudinal study of media coverage and public opinion on Chancellor Kohl," *International Journal of Public Opinion Research* 1 (1989), pp. 326–42.

14 Esteban Lopez-Escobar, Maxwell McCombs, and Antonio Tolsa, "Measuring the public images of political leaders: a methodological contribution of agenda-setting theory," paper presented to the Congreso do Investigación en Comunicación Politica, Madrid, Spain, 2007.

15 Spiro Kiousis and Maxwell McCombs, "Agenda-setting effects and attitude strength: political figures during the 1996 presidential election," *Communication Research* 31 (2004), pp. 36–57.

16 Tamir Sheafer, "The role of story evaluative tone in agenda setting and priming," *Journal of Communication* 57, 1 (2007), pp. 21–39.

17 Wayne Wanta, Guy Golan, and Cheolhan Lee, "Agenda setting and international news: media influence on public perceptions of foreign nations," *Journalism & Mass Communication Quarterly* 81 (2007), pp. 364–77.

18 Lynda Lee Kaid, "Political advertising," in *Encyclopedia of Political Communication*, ed. Lynda Lee Kaid and Christina Holtz-Bacha (Los Angeles, Calif.: Sage, 2008), pp. 563.

19 Renita Coleman and Stephen Banning, "Network TV news' affective framing of the presidential candidates: evidence for a second-level agenda-setting effect through visual framing," *Journalism & Mass Communication Quarterly* 83 (2006), pp. 313–28.

20 Drew Westen, *The Political Brain: The Role of Emotion in Deciding the Fate of the Nation* (New York: Public Affairs, 2007), p. ix (italics in original).

Chapter 9: Political Behavior

1 Bruce E. Pinkleton, Erica W. Austin, and Kristine K. J. Fortman, "Relationship of media use and political disaffection to political efficacy and voting behavior," *Journal of Broadcasting & Electronic Media* 42 (1998), pp. 34–49; John E. Jackson, "Election night reporting and voter turnout," *American Journal of Political Science* 30 (1983), pp. 212–25.

2 Paul Lazarsfeld, Bernard Berelson, and Hazel Gaudet, *The People's Choice* (New York: Columbia University Press, 1948).

3 Joohan Kim, Robert Wyatt, and Elihu Katz, "News, talk, opinion, participation: the part played by conversation in deliberative democracy," *Political Communication* 16 (1999), pp. 361–85.

4 Alex Tan, "Mass media use, issue knowledge, and political involvement," *Public Opinion Quarterly* 44 (1980), pp. 241–48.

5 Lyman A. Kellstedt, "The mass media and political behavior: television viewing habits and vote turnout," paper presented to the International Communication Association, Acapulco, Mexico, 1980.

6 Jack M. McLeod, Zhongshi Guo, Katie Daily, Catherine A. Steele, Huiping Huang, Edward Horowitz and Huailin Chen, "The impact of traditional and nontraditional media forms in the 1992 presidential election," *Journalism & Mass Communication Quarterly* 73 (1996), pp. 401–16.

7 William P. Eveland and Dietram A. Scheufele, "Connecting news media use with gaps in knowledge and participation," *Political Communication* 17 (2000), pp. 215–37.

8 Jack McLeod, Dietram A. Scheufele, and Patricia Moy, "Community, communication and participation: the role of mass media and interpersonal discussion in local political participation," *Political Communication* 16 (1999), pp. 315–36.

9 Dan Drew and David Weaver, "Voter learning in the 2004 Presidential Election: did the media matter?," *Journalism & Mass Communication Quarterly* 83 (2006), pp. 25–42.

10 Sei-Hill Kim and Miejeong Han, "Media use and participatory democracy in South Korea," *Mass Communication & Society* 8 (2005), pp. 133–53.

11 Thomas E. Patterson, *Out of Order* (New York: Knopf, 1993), p. 93.

12 Robert Putnam, *Bowling Alone: The Collapse and Revival of American Community* (New York: Simon & Schuster, 2000), p. 205.

13 Erik P. Bucy and Kimberly S. Gregson, "Media participation: a legitimizing mechanism of mass democracy," *New Media Society* 3 (2001), pp. 357–80.

14 Caroline Tolbert and Ramona S. McNeal, "Unraveling the effects of the internet on political participation?," *Political Research Quarterly* 56 (2003), pp. 175–85.

15 Gang Han, "New media use, sociodemographics, and voter turnout in the 2000 presidential election," *Mass Communication & Society* 11 (2008), pp. 62–81.

16 Stefano DellaVigna and Ethan Kaplan, "The Fox News effect: media bias and voting," *Quarterly Journal of Economics* 122 (2007), pp. 1187–1234.

17 Malcolm Brynin and Kenneth Newton, "The national press and voter turnout: general elections of 1992 and 1997," *Political Communication* 20 (2003), pp. 59–66.

18 Thomas M. Holbrook, *Do Campaigns Matter?* (London: Sage, 1996).

19 Stephen Ansolabehere, Rebecca Lessem and James M. Snyder, Jr., "The orientation of newspaper endorsements in U.S. elections, 1940–2002," *Quarterly Journal of Political Science* 1, 4 (2006), pp. 393–415.

20 James N. Druckman and Michael Parkin, "The impact of media bias: how editorial slant affects voters," *Journal of Politics* 67 (2005), pp. 1030–49.

21 Markus Prior, *Post-Broadcast Democracy: How Media Choice Increases Inequality in Political Involvement and Polarizes Elections* (New York: Cambridge University Press, 2007).

22 James N. Druckman, "Priming the vote," *Political Psychology* 25 (2004), pp. 577–94.

23 Matthew Mendelsohn, "The media and interpersonal communications: the priming of issues, leaders, and party identification," *Journal of Politics* 58 (1996), pp. 112–25; Tamir Sheafer and Gabriel Weimann, "Agenda building, agenda setting, priming, individual voting intentions, and the aggregate results: an analysis of four Israeli elections," *Journal of Communication* 55 (2005), pp. 247–365.

24 Spiro Kiousis and Michael McDevitt, "Agenda setting in civic development: effects of curricula and issue importance on youth voter turnout," *Communication Research* 35 (2008), pp. 481–502.

25 Marilyn S. Roberts, "Predicting voting behavior via the agenda setting tradition," *Journalism Quarterly* 69 (1992), pp. 878–92; and "Political advertising's influence on news, the public and their behavior," in *Communication and Democracy*, ed. Maxwell McCombs, Donald L. Shaw, and David H. Weaver (Mahwah, N.J.: Lawrence Erlbaum, 1997), pp. 85–98.

26 Michael X. Delli Carpini, "Mediating democratic engagement: the impact of communications on citizens involvement in political and civic life," in *Handbook of Political Communication Research*, ed. Lynda Lee Kaid (Mahwah, N.J.: Lawrence Erlbaum, 2004), pp. 395–434. Quote on p. 418 (emphasis in original).

27 Kenneth Fleming, Esther Thorson, and Zengjun Peng, "Associational membership as a source of social capital: its links to use of local newspaper, interpersonal communication, entertainment media, and volunteering," *Mass Communication and Society* 8 (2005), pp. 219–40.

28 Kenneth Fleming and Esther Thorson, "Assessing the role of information-processing strategies in learning from local news media about sources of social capital," *Mass Communication & Society* 11 (2008), pp. 398–419.

29 Keith Stamm and Robert Weis, "The newspaper and community integration: a study of ties to a local church community," *Communication Research* 13 (1986), pp. 125–37.

30 David H. Weaver, "Issue salience and public opinion: are there consequences of agenda-setting?" *International Journal of Public Opinion Research* 3 (1991), pp. 53–68.

31 Pippa Norris, "Does television erode social capital? A reply to Putnam," *PS: Political Science and Politics* 29 (1996), pp. 474–80.

32 Michael Xenos and Patricia Moy, "Direct and differential effects of the internet on political and civic engagement," *Journal of Communication* 57 (2007), pp. 704–18.

33 John E. Newhagen, "Media use and political efficacy: the suburbanization of race and class," *Journal of the American Society for Information Science* 45 (1994), pp. 386–94.

34 Diana Mutz, *Hearing the Other Side: Deliberative versus Participatory Democracy* (New York: Cambridge University Press, 2006).

35 Josh Pasek, Kate Kenski, Daniel Romer, and Kathleen Hall Jamieson, "America's youth and community engagement: how use of mass media is related to civic activity and political awareness in 14- to 22-year-olds," *Communication Research* 33 (2006), pp. 115–35.

36 Michael P. Boyle and Mike Schmierbach, "Media use and protest: the role of mainstream and alternative media in predicting mainstream and protest participation," *Communication Quarterly* 57 (2009), pp. 1–17.

37 Michael P. Boyle, Michael R. McCluskey, Douglas M. McLeod, and Sue E. Stein, "Newspapers and protest: an examination of protest coverage from 1960 to 1999," *Journalism & Mass Communication Quarterly* 82 (2005), pp. 638–53.

38 Mojan J. Dutta-Bergman, "Community participation and internet use after September 11: complementarity in channel consumption," *Journal of Computer-Mediated Communication* 11 (2004), http://jcmc.indiana.edu/vol11/issue2/dutta-bergman.html.

39 Hyunseo Hwang, Michael Schmierbach, Hye-Jin Paek, Homero Gil de Zuniga, and Dhavan V. Shah, "Media dissociation, internet use, and anti-war political participation," *Mass Communication and Society* 9 (2006), pp. 461–83.

40 Gadi Wolfsfeld, *Media and Political Conflict: News from the Middle East* (Cambridge, U.K.: Cambridge University Press, 1997).

41 Gustavo Cardoso and Pedro Pereira Neto, "Mass media driven mobilization and online protest: ICTs and the pro-East Timor movement in Portugal," in *Cyberprotest: New Media, Citizens, and Social Movements*, ed. Wim B. H. J. van de Donk, Brian D. Loader, Paul G. Nixon, and Dieter Rucht (London: Routledge, 2004), pp. 147–63.

42 Nojin Kwak, Nathaniel Poor, and Marko Skoric, "Honey, I shrunk the world! The relationship between internet use and international engagement," *Mass Communication and Society* 9 (2006), pp. 189–213.

43 Jesper Stromback and Lynda Lee Kaid, "A framework for comparing election news coverage around the world," in *The Handbook of Election News Coverage around the World*, ed. Jesper Stromback and Lynda Lee Kaid (London: Routledge, 2008), pp. 1–20.

Chapter 10: What Citizens Bring to the News

1 Fred N. Kerlinger, *Foundations of Behavioral Research*, 3rd ed. (New York: Harcourt Brace Jovanovich, 1986).

2 Virginia Dodge Fielder and Leonard P. Tipton, *Minorities and Newspapers* (Washington, D.C.: American Society of Newspaper Editors, 1986).

3 Gilbert Cranberg and Vincent Rodriguez, "The myth of the minority reader," *Columbia Journalism Review* 32 (1995), p. 42.

4 Gerald Stone, *Examining Newspapers: What Research Reveals About American Newspapers* (Beverly Hills, Calif.: Sage, 1987).

5 John H. Evans, "Religion and human cloning: an exploratory analysis of the first available opinion data," *Journal for the Scientific Study of Religion* 41 (2002), pp. 747–58.

6 Elihu Katz, Jay Blumler, and Michael Gurevitch, "Utilization of mass communication by the individual," in *The Uses of Mass Communication: Current Perspectives on Gratifications Research*, ed. Jay G. Blumler and Elihu Katz (Beverly Hills and London: Sage, 1974), pp. 19–33.

7 Phillip Palmgreen, "Uses and gratifications: a theoretical perspective," in *Communication Yearbook* 8, ed. Robert N. Bostrom (Beverly Hills, Calif.: Sage, 1984), pp. 20–55.

8 Barbara Kaye and Thomas J. Johnson, "Online and in the know: uses and gratifications of the web for political information," *Journal of Broadcasting & Electronic Media* 56 (2002), pp. 54–71.

9 Dhavan Shah, Nojin Kwak, and R. Lance Holbert, "'Connecting' and 'disconnecting' with civic life: patterns of internet use and the production of social capital," *Political Communication* 18 (2001), pp. 141–62.

10 David H. Weaver, "Audience need for orientation and media effects," *Communication Research* 7 (1980), pp. 361–77.

11 Jörg Matthes, "Need for orientation as a predictor of agenda-setting effects: causal evidence from a two-wave panel study," *International Journal of Public Opinion Research* 20 (2008), pp. 440–53.

12 Sandra Ball-Rokeach and Melvin DeFleur, "A dependency model of mass media effects," *Communication Research* 3 (1976), pp. 3–21.

13 Albert H. Hastorf and Hadley Cantril, "They saw a game: a case study," *Journal of Abnormal and Social Psychology* 49 (1954), pp. 129–34.

14 Natalie Jomini Stroud, "Polarization and partisan selective exposure," *Journal of Communication* 60 (2010), pp. 556–76.

15 Mira Sotirovic and Jack M. McLeod, "Knowledge as understanding: the information processing approach to political learning," in *Handbook of Political Communication Research*, ed. Lynda L. Kaid (Mahwah, N.J.: Lawrence Erlbaum, 2004), pp. 357–94.

16 Wayne Wanta, *The Public and the National Agenda: How People Learn about Important Issues* (Mahwah, N.J.: Lawrence Erlbaum, 1997).

17 Ran Wei and Ven H. Lo, "News media use and knowledge about the 2006 U.S. midterm elections: why exposure matters in voter learning," *International Journal of Public Opinion Research* 20, 3 (2008), pp. 347–62.

Chapter 11: News Influence on Civic Life

1 Walter Lippmann, *Public Opinion* (New York: Macmillan, 1922).

2 Michael Schudson, *The Good Citizen: A History of American Civic Life* (New York: Martin Kessler Books, 1998).

3 Samuel L. Popkin, *The Reasoning Voter: Communication and Persuasion in Presidential Campaigns* (Chicago: University of Chicago Press, 1991).

4 Anthony Downs, *An Economic Theory of Democracy* (New York: Harper & Row, 1957).

5 Benjamin I. Page and Robert Y. Shapiro, *The Rational Public: Fifty Years of Trends in Americans' Policy Preferences* (Chicago: University of Chicago Press, 1992).

6 R. Lance Holbert, R. Kelly Garrett, and Laurel S. Gleason, "A new era of minimal effects? A response to Bennett and Iyengar," *Journal of Communication* 60 (2010), pp. 15–34; R. Kelly Garrett, "Politically motivated reinforcement seeking: reframing the selective exposure debate," *Journal of Communication* 59 (2009), pp. 676–99.

7 W. Lance Bennett and Shanto Iyengar, "A new era of minimal effects? The changing foundations of political communication," *Journal of Communication* 58 (2008), pp. 707–31.

8 Michael Schudson, "The public journalism movement and its problems," in *The Politics of News: The News of Politics*, ed. Doris Graber, Denis McQuail, and Pippa Norris (Washington, D.C.: Congressional Quarterly, 1998), pp. 132–49.

9 Paul F. Lazarsfeld and Robert K. Merton, "Mass communication, popular taste and organized social action," in *The Communication of Ideas*, ed. Lyman Bryson (New York: Institute for Religious and Social Studies, 1948), pp. 95–118.

10 Anthony Downs, "Up and down with ecology: the 'issue-attention' cycle," *Public Interest* 28 (1972), pp. 38–50.

11 Jack M. McLeod and Byron Reeves, "On the nature of mass media effects," in *Television and Social Behavior: Beyond Violence and Children*, ed. Stephen B. Withey and Ronald P. Abeles Withey (Hillsdale, N.J.: Lawrence Erlbaum), pp. 17–54.

12 Spiro Kiousis and Maxwell E. McCombs, "Agenda-setting effects and attitude strength: political figures during the 1996 presidential election," *Communication Research* 31 (2004), pp. 36–57.

Chapter 12. An Assessment of the News in Democratic Life

1 Lester Milbrath, *Political Participation* (Chicago: Rand McNally, 1965).

2 Robert W. McChesney, *Rich Media, Poor Democracy: Communication Politics in Dubious Times* (Urbana: University of Illinois Press, 1999).

3 Alexandra Kitty and Robert Greenwald, *Outfoxed: Rupert Murdoch's War on Journalism* (St. Paul, Minn.: Disinformation, 2005).

4 Jay Rosen, *Getting the Connections Right: Public Journalism and the Troubles in the Press* (New York: Twentieth Century Fund, 1996).

5 R. Lance Holbert and Stephen J. Zubric, "A comparative analysis of objective and public journalism as techniques," *Newspaper Research Journal* 21 (2000), pp. 50–67.

6 W. Lance Bennett and Shanto Iyengar, "A new era of minimal effects? The changing foundations of political communication," *Journal of Communication* 58 (2008), pp. 707–31.

7 R. Lance Holbert, R. Kelly Garrett, and Laurel S. Gleason, "A new era of minimal effects? A response to Bennett and Iyengar," *Journal of Communication* 60 (2010), pp. 15–34.

8 Michael Schudson, *The Power of News* (Cambridge, Mass.: Harvard University Press, 1995).

9 Harold D. Lasswell, *Propaganda Technique in the World War* (New York: A. A. Knopf, 1927).

10 Bennett and Iyengar, "A new era of minimal effects?"

11 R. Kelly Garrett, "Politically motivated reinforcement seeking: reframing the selective exposure debate," *Journal of Communication* 59 (2009), pp. 676–99.

12 Margaret A. Blanchard, *The Hutchins Commission: The Press and the Responsibility Concept* (Lexington, Ky.: Association for Education in Journalism, 1977).

13 James S. Ettema, "Journalism as reason-giving: deliberative democracy, insti-
tutional   accountability,   and   the   new   media's   mission,"   *Political
Communication* 24 (2007), pp. 143–60.

Index

199

Index

Index

Index

Index

Index

CPSIA information can be obtained
at www.ICGtesting.com
Printed in the USA
JSHW031934170822
29204JS00006B/59